I0007241

Amazon Kinesis Firehose Developer Guide

A catalogue record for this book is available from the Hong Kong Public Libraries.

Published in Hong Kong by Samurai Media Limited.

Email: info@samuraimedia.org

ISBN 9789888407965

Copyright 2018 Amazon Web Services, Inc. and/or its affiliates.
Minor modifications for publication Copyright 2018 Samurai Media Limited.

This book is licensed under the Creative Commons Attribution-ShareAlike 4.0 International Public License.

Background Cover Image by https://www.flickr.com/people/webtreatsetc/

Contents

What Is Amazon Kinesis Data Firehose?

Amazon Kinesis Data Firehose is a fully managed service for delivering real-time streaming data to destinations such as Amazon Simple Storage Service (Amazon S3), Amazon Redshift, Amazon Elasticsearch Service (Amazon ES), and Splunk. Kinesis Data Firehose is part of the Kinesis streaming data platform, along with Kinesis Streams and Amazon Kinesis Data Analytics. With Kinesis Data Firehose, you don't need to write applications or manage resources. You configure your data producers to send data to Kinesis Data Firehose, and it automatically delivers the data to the destination that you specified. You can also configure Kinesis Data Firehose to transform your data before delivering it.

For more information about AWS big data solutions, see Big Data. For more information about AWS streaming data solutions, see What is Streaming Data?

Key Concepts

As you get started with Kinesis Data Firehose, you'll benefit from understanding the following concepts:

Kinesis data delivery stream
The underlying entity of Kinesis Data Firehose. You use Kinesis Data Firehose by creating a Kinesis data delivery stream and then sending data to it. For more information, see Creating an Amazon Kinesis Data Firehose Delivery Stream and Sending Data to an Amazon Kinesis Firehose Delivery Stream.

record
The data of interest that your data producer sends to a Kinesis data delivery stream. A record can be as large as 1,000 KB.

data producer
Producers send records to Kinesis data delivery streams. For example, a web server that sends log data to a Kinesis data delivery stream is a data producer. You can also configure your Kinesis data delivery stream to automatically read data from an existing Kinesis stream, and load it into destinations. For more information, see Sending Data to an Amazon Kinesis Firehose Delivery Stream.

buffer size and buffer interval
Kinesis Data Firehose buffers incoming streaming data to a certain size or for a certain period of time before delivering it to destinations. Buffer Size is in MBs and Buffer Interval is in seconds.

Data Flow

For Amazon S3 destinations, streaming data is delivered to your S3 bucket. If data transformation is enabled, you can optionally back up source data to another Amazon S3 bucket.

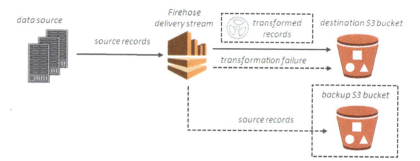

For Amazon Redshift destinations, streaming data is delivered to your S3 bucket first. Kinesis Data Firehose then issues an Amazon Redshift COPY command to load data from your S3 bucket to your Amazon Redshift cluster. If data transformation is enabled, you can optionally back up source data to another Amazon S3 bucket.

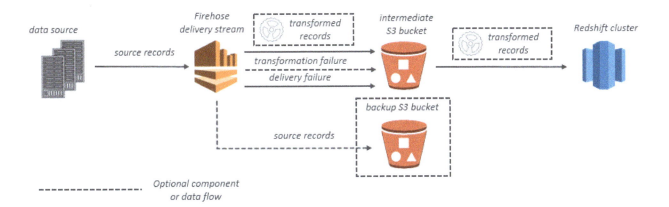

For Amazon ES destinations, streaming data is delivered to your Amazon ES cluster, and it can optionally be backed up to your S3 bucket concurrently.

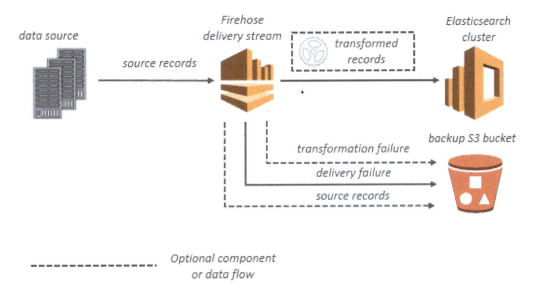

For Splunk destinations, streaming data is delivered to Splunk, and it can optionally be backed up to your S3 bucket concurrently.

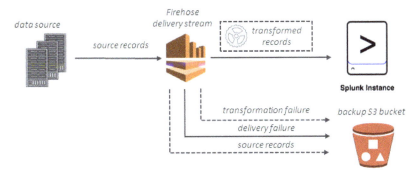

Setting Up for Amazon Kinesis Data Firehose

Before you use Kinesis Data Firehose for the first time, complete the following tasks.

Topics

- Sign Up for AWS
- Optional: Download Libraries and Tools

Sign Up for AWS

When you sign up for Amazon Web Services (AWS), your AWS account is automatically signed up for all services in AWS, including Kinesis Data Firehose. You are charged only for the services that you use.

If you have an AWS account already, skip to the next task. If you don't have an AWS account, use the following procedure to create one.

To sign up for an AWS account

1. Open https://aws.amazon.com/, and then choose **Create an AWS Account**. **Note**
   This might be unavailable in your browser if you previously signed into the AWS Management Console. In that case, choose **Sign in to a different account**, and then choose **Create a new AWS account**.

2. Follow the online instructions.

   Part of the sign-up procedure involves receiving a phone call and entering a PIN using the phone keypad.

Optional: Download Libraries and Tools

The following libraries and tools will help you work with Kinesis Data Firehose programmatically and from the command line:

- The Amazon Kinesis Firehose API Reference is the basic set of operations that Kinesis Data Firehose supports.

- The AWS SDKs for Java, .NET, Node.js, Python, and Ruby include Kinesis Data Firehose support and samples.

   If your version of the AWS SDK for Java does not include samples for Kinesis Data Firehose, you can also download the latest AWS SDK from GitHub.

- The AWS Command Line Interface supports Kinesis Data Firehose. The AWS CLI enables you to control multiple AWS services from the command line and automate them through scripts.

Creating an Amazon Kinesis Data Firehose Delivery Stream

You can use the AWS Management Console or an AWS SDK to create a Kinesis data delivery stream to your chosen destination.

You can update the configuration of your Kinesis data delivery stream at any time after it's created, using the Kinesis Data Firehose console or UpdateDestination. Your Kinesis data delivery stream remains in the `ACTIVE` state while your configuration is updated, and you can continue to send data. The updated configuration normally takes effect within a few minutes. The version number of a Kinesis data delivery stream is increased by a value of 1 after you update the configuration, and it is reflected in the delivered Amazon S3 object name. For more information, see Amazon S3 Object Name Format.

The following topics describe how to create a Kinesis data delivery stream:

Topics

- Name and source
- Transform records
- Choose destination
- Configure settings

Name and source

This topic describes the **Name and source** page of the **Create Delivery Stream** wizard.

Name and source

1. Open the Kinesis Firehose console at https://console.aws.amazon.com/firehose/.

2. Choose **Create Delivery Stream**. On the **Name and source** page, enter values for the following fields:
   Delivery stream name
   The name of your Kinesis data delivery stream.
   Source

   - **Direct PUT or other sources:** Choose this option to create a Kinesis data delivery stream that producer applications write directly to.
   - **Kinesis stream:** Choose this option to configure a Kinesis data delivery stream that uses a Kinesis stream as a data source. You can then use Amazon Kinesis Data Firehose to read data easily from an existing Kinesis stream and load it into destinations. For more information about using Kinesis Data Streams as your data source, see Writing to Amazon Kinesis Data Firehose Using Kinesis Data Streams.

3. Choose **Next** to advance to the Transform records page.

Transform records

This topic describes the **Transform records** page of the **Create Delivery Stream** wizard.

Transform records

1. On the **Transform records with AWS Lambda** page, enter values for the following fields:
   Record transformation
   Choose **Disabled** to create a Kinesis data delivery stream that does not transform incoming data. Choose **Enabled** to specify a Lambda function that Kinesis Data Firehose can invoke to transform incoming data before delivering it. You can configure a new Lambda function using one of the Lambda blueprints or choose an existing Lambda function. Your Lambda function must contain the status model required by Kinesis Data Firehose. For more information, see Amazon Kinesis Data Firehose Data Transformation.

2. Choose **Next** to advance to the Choose destination page.

Choose destination

This topic describes the **Choose destination** page of the **Create Delivery Stream** wizard.

Amazon Kinesis Data Firehose can send records to Amazon S3, Amazon Redshift, or Amazon Elasticsearch Service.

Topics

- Choose Amazon S3 for Your Destination
- Choose Amazon Redshift for Your Destination
- Choose Amazon ES for Your Destination
- Choose Splunk for Your Destination

Choose Amazon S3 for Your Destination

This section describes options for using Amazon S3 for your destination.

To choose Amazon S3 for your destination

- On the **Choose destination** page, enter values for the following fields:
  Destination
  Choose **Amazon S3**.
  Destination S3 bucket
  Choose an S3 bucket that you own where the streaming data should be delivered. You can create a new S3 bucket or choose an existing one.
  Destination S3 bucket prefix
  (Optional) To use the default prefix for S3 objects, leave this option blank. Kinesis Data Firehose automatically uses a prefix in "YYYY/MM/DD/HH" UTC time format for delivered S3 objects. You can add to the start of this prefix. For more information, see Amazon S3 Object Name Format.
  Source record S3 backup
  Choose **Disabled** to disable source record backup. If you enable data transformation with Lambda, you can enable source record backup to deliver untransformed incoming data to a separate S3 bucket. You can add to the start of the "YYYY/MM/DD/HH" UTC time prefix generated by Kinesis Data Firehose. You cannot disable source record backup after you enable it.

Choose Amazon Redshift for Your Destination

This section describes options for using Amazon Redshift for your destination.

To choose Amazon Redshift for your destination

- On the **Choose destination** page, enter values for the following fields:
  Destination
  Choose **Amazon Redshift**.
  Cluster
  The Amazon Redshift cluster to which S3 bucket data is copied. Configure the Amazon Redshift cluster to be publicly accessible and unblock Kinesis Data Firehose IP addresses. For more information, see Grant Kinesis Data Firehose Access to an Amazon Redshift Destination .
  User name
  An Amazon Redshift user with permissions to access the Amazon Redshift cluster. This user needs to have the Amazon Redshift `INSERT` privilege for copying data from the S3 bucket to the Amazon Redshift cluster.
  Password
  The password for the user who has permissions to access the cluster.
  Database
  The Amazon Redshift database to where the data is copied.

Table

The Amazon Redshift table to where the data is copied.

Columns

(Optional) The specific columns of the table to which the data is copied. Use this option if the number of columns defined in your S3 objects is less than the number of columns within the Amazon Redshift table.

Intermediate S3 bucket Kinesis Data Firehose delivers your data to your S3 bucket first and then issues an Amazon Redshift COPY command to load the data into your Amazon Redshift cluster. Specify an S3 bucket that you own where the streaming data should be delivered. Create a new S3 bucket or choose an existing bucket that you own.

Kinesis Data Firehose doesn't delete the data from your S3 bucket after loading it to your Amazon Redshift cluster. You can manage the data in your S3 bucket using a lifecycle configuration. For more information, see Object Lifecycle Management in the *Amazon Simple Storage Service Developer Guide*.

Intermediate S3 bucket prefix

(Optional) To use the default prefix for S3 objects, leave this option blank. Kinesis Data Firehose automatically uses a prefix in "YYYY/MM/DD/HH" UTC time format for delivered S3 objects. You can add to the start of this prefix. For more information, see Amazon S3 Object Name Format.

COPY options Parameters that you can specify in the Amazon Redshift COPY command. These may be required for your configuration. For example, "GZIP" is required if S3 data compression is enabled; "REGION" is required if your S3 bucket isn't in the same AWS Region as your Amazon Redshift cluster. For more information, see COPY in the *Amazon Redshift Database Developer Guide*.

COPY command The Amazon Redshift COPY command. For more information, see COPY in the *Amazon Redshift Database Developer Guide*.

Retry duration

Time duration (0–7200 seconds) for Kinesis Data Firehose to retry if data COPY to your Amazon Redshift cluster fails. Kinesis Firehose retries every 5 minutes until the retry duration ends. If you set the retry duration to 0 (zero) seconds, Kinesis Data Firehose does not retry upon a COPY command failure.

Source record S3 backup If you enable data transformation with Lambda, you can enable source record backup to deliver untransformed incoming data to a separate S3 bucket. You cannot disable source record backup after you enable it.

Backup S3 bucket

The S3 bucket to receive the untransformed data.

Backup S3 bucket prefix

To use the default prefix for source record backup, leave this option blank. Kinesis Data Firehose automatically uses a prefix in "YYYY/MM/DD/HH" UTC time format for delivered S3 objects. You can add to the start of this prefix. For more information, see Amazon S3 Object Name Format. This value is optional.

Choose Amazon ES for Your Destination

This section describes options for using Amazon ES for your destination.

To choose Amazon ES for your destination

1. On the **Choose destination** page, enter values for the following fields:

   Destination

   Choose **Amazon Elasticsearch Service**.

   Domain

   The Amazon ES domain to which your data is delivered.

   Index

   The Elasticsearch index name to be used when indexing data to your Amazon ES cluster.

   Index rotation

   Choose whether and how often the Elasticsearch index should be rotated. If index rotation is enabled, Kinesis Firehose appends the corresponding time stamp to the specified index name and rotates. For more information, see Index Rotation for the Amazon ES Destination.

   Type

The Amazon ES type name to be used when indexing data to your Amazon ES cluster. For Elasticsearch 6.x, there can be only one type per index. If you try to specify a new type for an existing index which already has another type, Kinesis Firehose returns an error during runtime.

Retry duration

Time duration (0–7200 seconds) for Kinesis Firehose to retry if an index request to your Amazon ES cluster fails. Kinesis Firehose retries every 5 minutes until the retry duration ends. If you set the retry duration to 0 (zero) seconds, Kinesis Firehose does not retry upon an index request failure.

Backup mode

You can choose to either back up failed records only or all records. If you choose failed records only, any data that Kinesis Firehose could not deliver to your Amazon ES cluster or your Lambda function could not transform are backed up to the specified S3 bucket. If you choose all records, Kinesis Firehose backs up all incoming source data to your S3 bucket concurrently with data delivery to Amazon ES. For more information, see Data Delivery Failure Handling and Data Transformation Failure Handling.

Backup S3 bucket

An S3 bucket you own that is the target of the backup data. Create a new S3 bucket or choose an existing bucket that you own.

Backup S3 bucket prefix

(Optional) To use the default prefix for S3 objects, leave this option blank. Kinesis Data Firehose automatically uses a prefix in "YYYY/MM/DD/HH" UTC time format for delivered S3 objects. You can add to the start of this prefix. For more information, see Amazon S3 Object Name Format. This value is optional.

2. Choose **Next** to advance to the Configure settings page.

Choose Splunk for Your Destination

This section describes options for using Splunk for your destination.

To choose Splunk for your destination

- On the **Choose destination** page, enter values for the following fields:

  Destination

  Choose **Splunk**.

  Splunk cluster endpoint

  To determine the endpoint, see Configure Amazon Kinesis Firehose to Send Data to the Splunk Platform in the Splunk documentation.

  Splunk endpoint type

  Choose `Raw` in most cases. Choose `Event` if you have preprocessed your data using AWS Lambda in order to send data to different indexes by event type. For detailed information on what endpoint to use, see Configure Amazon Kinesis Firehose to Send Data to the Splunk Platform in the Splunk documentation.

  Authentication token

  To set up a Splunk endpoint that can receive data from Kinesis Firehose, follow the instructions at Installation and Configuration Overview for the Splunk Add-on for Amazon Kinesis Firehose in the Splunk documentation. Save the token that you get from Splunk when you set up the endpoint for this delivery stream, and add it here.

  HEC acknowledgement timeout

  Specify how long Kinesis Firehose waits for index acknowledgement from Splunk. If Splunk doesn't send the acknowledgment before the timeout is reached, Kinesis Firehose considers it a data delivery failure. Kinesis Firehose then either retries or backs up the data to your Amazon S3 bucket, depending on the retry duration value that you set.

  Retry duration

  Specify how long Kinesis Firehose retries sending data to Splunk.

  After sending data, Kinesis Firehose first waits for an acknowledgment from Splunk. If an error occurs or the acknowledgment doesn't arrive within the acknowledgment timeout period, Kinesis Firehose starts the retry duration counter. It keeps retrying until the retry duration expires, after which Kinesis Firehose considers it a data delivery failure and backs up the data to your Amazon S3 bucket.

Every time Kinesis Firehose sends data to Splunk, whether it's the initial attempt or a retry, it restarts the acknowledgement timeout counter and waits for an acknowledgement to arrive from Splunk.

Even if the retry duration expires, Kinesis Firehose still waits for the acknowledgment until it receives it or the acknowledgement timeout period is reached. If the acknowledgment times out, Kinesis Firehose determines whether there's time left in the retry counter. If there is time left, it retries again and repeats the logic until it receives an acknowledgment or determines that the retry time has expired.

If you don't want Kinesis Firehose to retry sending data, set this value to 0.

S3 backup mode

Choose whether to back up all the events that Kinesis Firehose sends to Splunk or only the ones for which delivery to Splunk fails. If you require high data durability, turn on this backup mode for all events. Also consider backing up all events initially, until you verify that your data is getting indexed correctly in Splunk.

S3 backup bucket

Choose an existing backup bucket or create a new one.

S3 backup bucket prefix

You can specify a prefix for your Amazon S3 backup bucket.

Configure settings

This topic describes the **Configure settings** page of the **Create Delivery Stream** wizard.

Configure settings

1. On the **Configure settings** page, enter values for the following fields:
   Buffer size, Buffer interval Kinesis Data Firehose buffers incoming data before delivering it to Amazon S3. You can choose a buffer size (1–128 MBs) or buffer interval (60–900 seconds); whichever condition is satisfied first triggers data delivery to Amazon S3. If you enable data transformation, the buffer interval applies from the time transformed data is received by Kinesis Data Firehose to the data delivery to Amazon S3. In circumstances where data delivery to the destination falls behind data writing to the delivery stream, Kinesis Data Firehose raises the buffer size dynamically to catch up and ensure that all data is delivered to the destination.
   Compression Choose GZIP, Snappy, or Zip data compression, or no data compression. Snappy or Zip compression are not available for delivery streams with Amazon Redshift as the destination.
   Encryption
   Kinesis Data Firehose supports Amazon S3 server-side encryption with AWS Key Management Service (AWS KMS) for encrypting delivered data in Amazon S3. You can choose to not encrypt the data or to encrypt with a key from the list of AWS KMS keys that you own. For more information, see Protecting Data Using Server-Side Encryption with AWS KMS–Managed Keys (SSE-KMS).
   Error logging
   Kinesis Data Firehose can log the Lambda invocation, if data transformation is enabled, and send data delivery errors to CloudWatch Logs so that you can view the specific error logs if the Lambda invocation or data delivery fails. For more information, see Monitoring with Amazon CloudWatch Logs.
   IAM role
   You can choose to create a new role where required permissions are assigned automatically, or choose an existing role created for Kinesis Data Firehose. The role is used to grant Kinesis Data Firehose access to your S3 bucket, AWS KMS key (if data encryption is enabled), and Lambda function (if data transformation is enabled). The console might create a role with placeholders. You can safely ignore or safely delete lines with %FIREHOSE_BUCKET_NAME%, %FIREHOSE_DEFAULT_FUNCTION%, or %FIREHOSE_DEFAULT_VERSION%. For more information, see Grant Kinesis Data Firehose Access to an Amazon S3 Destination.

2. Review the settings and choose **Create Delivery Stream**.

The new Kinesis data delivery stream takes a few moments in the **Creating** state before it is available. After your Kinesis data delivery stream is in an **Active** state, you can start sending data to it from your producer.

16

Testing Your Delivery Stream Using Sample Data

You can use the AWS Management Console to ingest simulated stock ticker data. The console runs a script in your browser to put sample records in your Kinesis Firehose delivery stream. This enables you to test the configuration of your delivery stream without having to generate your own test data.

The following is an example from the simulated data:

```
1 {"TICKER_SYMBOL":"QXZ","SECTOR":"HEALTHCARE","CHANGE":-0.05,"PRICE":84.51}
```

Note that standard Amazon Kinesis Firehose charges apply when your delivery stream transmits the data, but there is no charge when the data is generated. To stop incurring these charges, you can stop the sample stream from the console at any time.

Topics

- Prerequisites
- Test Using Amazon S3 as the Destination
- Test Using Amazon Redshift as the Destination
- Test Using Amazon ES as the Destination
- Test Using Splunk as the Destination

Prerequisites

Before you begin, create a delivery stream. For more information, see Creating an Amazon Kinesis Data Firehose Delivery Stream.

Test Using Amazon S3 as the Destination

Use the following procedure to test your delivery stream using Amazon Simple Storage Service (Amazon S3) as the destination.

To test a delivery stream using Amazon S3

1. Open the Kinesis Firehose console at https://console.aws.amazon.com/firehose/.

2. Choose the delivery stream.

3. Under **Test with demo data**, choose **Start sending demo data** to generate sample stock ticker data.

4. Follow the onscreen instructions to verify that data is being delivered to your S3 bucket. Note that it might take a few minutes for new objects to appear in your bucket, based on the buffering configuration of your bucket.

5. When the test is complete, choose **Stop sending demo data** to stop incurring usage charges.

Test Using Amazon Redshift as the Destination

Use the following procedure to test your delivery stream using Amazon Redshift as the destination.

To test a delivery stream using Amazon Redshift

1. Your delivery stream expects a table to be present in your Amazon Redshift cluster. Connect to Amazon Redshift through a SQL interface and run the following statement to create a table that accepts the sample data.

```
1 create table firehose_test_table
2 (
3   TICKER_SYMBOL varchar(4),
4   SECTOR varchar(16),
5   CHANGE float,
6   PRICE float
7 );
```

2. Open the Kinesis Firehose console at https://console.aws.amazon.com/firehose/.

3. Choose the delivery stream.

4. Edit the destination details for your delivery stream to point to the newly created `firehose_test_table` table.

5. Under **Test with demo data**, choose **Start sending demo data** to generate sample stock ticker data.

6. Follow the onscreen instructions to verify that data is being delivered to your table. Note that it might take a few minutes for new rows to appear in your table, based on the buffering configuration.

7. When the test is complete, choose **Stop sending demo data** to stop incurring usage charges.

8. Edit the destination details for your Kinesis Firehose delivery stream to point to another table.

9. (Optional) Delete the `firehose_test_table` table.

Test Using Amazon ES as the Destination

Use the following procedure to test your delivery stream using Amazon Elasticsearch Service (Amazon ES) as the destination.

To test a delivery stream using Amazon ES

1. Open the Kinesis Firehose console at https://console.aws.amazon.com/firehose/.

2. Choose the delivery stream.

3. Under **Test with demo data**, choose **Start sending demo data** to generate sample stock ticker data.

4. Follow the onscreen instructions to verify that data is being delivered to your Amazon ES domain. For more information, see Searching Documents in an Amazon ES Domain in the *Amazon Elasticsearch Service Developer Guide*.

5. When the test is complete, choose **Stop sending demo data** to stop incurring usage charges.

Test Using Splunk as the Destination

Use the following procedure to test your delivery stream using Splunk as the destination.

To test a delivery stream using Splunk

1. Open the Kinesis Firehose console at https://console.aws.amazon.com/firehose/.

2. Choose the delivery stream.

3. Under **Test with demo data**, choose **Start sending demo data** to generate sample stock ticker data.

4. Check whether the data is being delivered to your Splunk index. Example search terms in Splunk are `sourcetype="aws:firehose:json"` and `index="name-of-your-splunk-index"`. For more information about how to search for events in Splunk, see Search Manual in the Splunk documentation.

If the test data doesn't appear in your Splunk index, check your Amazon S3 bucket for failed events. Also see Data Not Delivered to Splunk.

5. When you finish testing, choose **Stop sending demo data** to stop incurring usage charges.

Sending Data to an Amazon Kinesis Firehose Delivery Stream

You can send data to your Kinesis data delivery stream using different types of sources: You can use a Kinesis stream, the Kinesis Agent, or the Kinesis Firehose API using the AWS SDK. You can also use Amazon CloudWatch Logs, CloudWatch Events, or AWS IoT as your data source. If you are new to Kinesis Firehose, take some time to become familiar with the concepts and terminology presented in What Is Amazon Kinesis Data Firehose?.

Note
Some AWS services can only send messages and events to a Kinesis Data Firehose delivery stream that is in the same Region. If your Kinesis Data Firehose delivery stream doesn't appear as an option when you're configuring a target for Amazon CloudWatch Logs, CloudWatch Events, or AWS IoT, verify that your Kinesis Data Firehose delivery stream is in the same Region as your other services.

Topics

- Writing to Amazon Kinesis Data Firehose Using Kinesis Data Streams
- Writing to Amazon Kinesis Data Firehose Using Kinesis Agent
- Writing to a Kinesis Data Delivery Stream Using the AWS SDK
- Writing to Amazon Kinesis Data Firehose Using CloudWatch Logs
- Writing to Amazon Kinesis Data Firehose Using CloudWatch Events
- Writing to Amazon Kinesis Data Firehose Using AWS IoT

Writing to Amazon Kinesis Data Firehose Using Kinesis Data Streams

You can configure Kinesis Data Streams to send information to a Kinesis Data Firehose delivery stream.

1. Open the Kinesis Firehose console at https://console.aws.amazon.com/firehose/.

2. Choose **Create Delivery Stream**. On the **Name and source** page, enter values for the following fields:
   Delivery stream name
   The name of your Kinesis data delivery stream.
   Source
   Choose the **Kinesis stream** option to configure a Kinesis data delivery stream that uses a Kinesis stream as a data source. You can then use Amazon Kinesis Data Firehose to read data easily from an existing Kinesis stream and load it into destinations.
   To use a Kinesis stream as a source, choose an existing stream in the **Kinesis stream** list, or choose **Create new** to create a new Kinesis stream. After you create a new stream, choose **Refresh** to update the **Kinesis stream** list. If you have a large number of streams, filter the list using **Filter by name**.
   When you configure a Kinesis stream as the source of a Kinesis Data Firehose delivery stream, the Kinesis Data Firehose `PutRecord` and `PutRecordBatch` operations are disabled. To add data to your Kinesis Data Firehose delivery stream in this case, use the Kinesis Data Streams `PutRecord` and `PutRecords` operations. Kinesis Data Firehose starts reading data from the `LATEST` position of your Kinesis stream. For more information about Kinesis Data Streams positions, see GetShardIterator. Kinesis Data Firehose calls the Kinesis Data Streams GetRecords operation once per second for each shard.
   More than one Kinesis Data Firehose delivery stream can read from the same Kinesis stream. Other Kinesis applications (consumers) can also read from the same stream. Each call from any Kinesis Data Firehose delivery stream or other consumer application counts against the overall throttling limit for the shard. To avoid getting throttled, plan your applications carefully. For more information about Kinesis Data Streams limits, see Amazon Kinesis Streams Limits.

3. Choose **Next** to advance to the Transform records page.

Writing to Amazon Kinesis Data Firehose Using Kinesis Agent

Kinesis Agent is a stand-alone Java software application that offers an easy way to collect and send data to Kinesis Data Firehose. The agent continuously monitors a set of files and sends new data to your Kinesis data delivery stream. The agent handles file rotation, checkpointing, and retry upon failures. It delivers all of your data in a reliable, timely, and simple manner. It also emits Amazon CloudWatch metrics to help you better monitor and troubleshoot the streaming process.

By default, records are parsed from each file based on the newline ('\n') character. However, the agent can also be configured to parse multi-line records (see Agent Configuration Settings).

You can install the agent on Linux-based server environments such as web servers, log servers, and database servers. After installing the agent, configure it by specifying the files to monitor and the delivery stream for the data. After the agent is configured, it durably collects data from the files and reliably sends it to the delivery stream.

Topics

- Prerequisites
- Download and Install the Agent
- Configure and Start the Agent
- Agent Configuration Settings
- Monitor Multiple File Directories and Write to Multiple Streams
- Use the Agent to Pre-process Data
- Agent CLI Commands

Prerequisites

- Your operating system must be either Amazon Linux AMI with version 2015.09 or later, or Red Hat Enterprise Linux version 7 or later.
- If you are using Amazon EC2 to run your agent, launch your EC2 instance.
- Manage your AWS credentials using one of the following methods:
    - Specify an IAM role when you launch your EC2 instance.
    - Specify AWS credentials when you configure the agent (see awsAccessKeyId and awsSecretAccessKey).
    - Edit /etc/sysconfig/aws-kinesis-agent to specify your region and AWS access keys.
    - If your EC2 instance is in a different AWS account, create an IAM role to provide access to the Kinesis Data Firehose service, and specify that role when you configure the agent (see assumeRoleARN and assumeRoleExternalId). Use one of the previous methods to specify the AWS credentials of a user in the other account who has permission to assume this role.
- The IAM role or AWS credentials that you specify must have permission to perform the Kinesis Data Firehose PutRecordBatch operation for the agent to send data to your delivery stream. If you enable CloudWatch monitoring for the agent, permission to perform the CloudWatch PutMetricData operation is also needed. For more information, see Controlling Access with Amazon Kinesis Data Firehose , Monitoring Kinesis Agent Health, and Authentication and Access Control for Amazon CloudWatch.

Download and Install the Agent

First, connect to your instance. For more information, see Connect to Your Instance in the *Amazon EC2 User Guide for Linux Instances*. If you have trouble connecting, see Troubleshooting Connecting to Your Instance in the *Amazon EC2 User Guide for Linux Instances*.

Next, install the agent using one of the following methods.

To set up the agent using the Amazon Linux AMI
Use the following command to download and install the agent:

```
1 sudo yum install -y aws-kinesis-agent
```

To set up the agent using Red Hat Enterprise Linux
Use the following command to download and install the agent:

```
1 sudo yum install -y https://s3.amazonaws.com/streaming-data-agent/aws-kinesis-agent-latest.amzn1
    .noarch.rpm
```

To set up the agent using GitHub

1. Download the agent from awslabs/amazon-kinesis-agent.

2. Install the agent by navigating to the download directory and running the following command:

```
1 sudo ./setup --install
```

Configure and Start the Agent

To configure and start the agent

1. Open and edit the configuration file (as superuser if using default file access permissions): `/etc/aws-kinesis/agent.json`

   In this configuration file, specify the files (`"filePattern"`) from which the agent collects data, and the name of the delivery stream (`"deliveryStream"`) to which the agent sends data. Note that the file name is a pattern, and the agent recognizes file rotations. You can rotate files or create new files no more than once per second. The agent uses the file creation timestamp to determine which files to track and tail into your delivery stream; creating new files or rotating files more frequently than once per second does not allow the agent to differentiate properly between them.

```
1 {
2     "flows": [
3         {
4             "filePattern": "/tmp/app.log*",
5             "deliveryStream": "yourdeliverystream"
6         }
7     ]
8 }
```

   Note that the default region is `us-east-1`. If you are using a different region, add the `firehose.endpoint` setting to the configuration file, specifying the endpoint for your region. For more information, see Agent Configuration Settings.

2. Start the agent manually:

```
1 sudo service aws-kinesis-agent start
```

3. (Optional) Configure the agent to start on system startup:

```
1 sudo chkconfig aws-kinesis-agent on
```

The agent is now running as a system service in the background. It continuously monitors the specified files and sends data to the specified delivery stream. Agent activity is logged in `/var/log/aws-kinesis-agent/aws-kinesis-agent.log`.

Agent Configuration Settings

The agent supports two mandatory configuration settings, `filePattern` and `deliveryStream`, plus optional configuration settings for additional features. You can specify both mandatory and optional configuration settings in `/etc/aws-kinesis/agent.json`.

Whenever you change the configuration file, you must stop and start the agent, using the following commands:

```
1 sudo service aws-kinesis-agent stop
2 sudo service aws-kinesis-agent start
```

Alternatively, you could use the following command:

```
1 sudo service aws-kinesis-agent restart
```

The following are the general configuration settings.

Configuration Setting	Description
assumeRoleARN	The ARN of the role to be assumed by the user. For more information, see Delegate Access Across AWS Accounts Using IAM Roles in the *IAM User Guide*.
assumeRoleExternalId	An optional identifier that determines who can assume the role. For more information, see How to Use an External ID in the *IAM User Guide*.
awsAccessKeyId	AWS access key ID that overrides the default credentials. This setting takes precedence over all other credential providers.
awsSecretAccessKey	AWS secret key that overrides the default credentials. This setting takes precedence over all other credential providers.
cloudwatch.emitMetrics	Enables the agent to emit metrics to CloudWatch if set (true). Default: true
cloudwatch.endpoint	The regional endpoint for CloudWatch. Default: `monitoring.us-east-1.amazonaws.com`
firehose.endpoint	The regional endpoint for Kinesis Data Firehose. Default: `firehose.us-east-1.amazonaws.com`

The following are the flow configuration settings.

Configuration Setting	Description
dataProcessingOptions	The list of processing options applied to each parsed record before it is sent to the delivery stream. The processing options are performed in the specified order. For more information, see Use the Agent to Pre-process Data.
deliveryStream	[Required] The name of the delivery stream.

Configuration Setting	Description
filePattern	[Required] A glob for the files that need to be monitored by the agent. Any file that matches this pattern is picked up by the agent automatically and monitored. For all files matching this pattern, read permission must be granted to `aws-kinesis-agent-user`. For the directory containing the files, read and execute permissions must be granted to `aws-kinesis-agent-user`.
initialPosition	The initial position from which the file started to be parsed. Valid values are `START_OF_FILE` and `END_OF_FILE`. Default: `END_OF_FILE`
maxBufferAgeMillis	The maximum time, in milliseconds, for which the agent buffers data before sending it to the delivery stream. Value range: 1,000 to 900,000 (1 second to 15 minutes) Default: 60,000 (1 minute)
maxBufferSizeBytes	The maximum size, in bytes, for which the agent buffers data before sending it to the delivery stream. Value range: 1 to 4,194,304 (4 MB) Default: 4,194,304 (4 MB)
maxBufferSizeRecords	The maximum number of records for which the agent buffers data before sending it to the delivery stream. Value range: 1 to 500 Default: 500
minTimeBetweenFilePollsMillis	The time interval, in milliseconds, at which the agent polls and parses the monitored files for new data. Value range: 1 or more Default: 100
multiLineStartPattern	The pattern for identifying the start of a record. A record is made of a line that matches the pattern and any following lines that don't match the pattern. The valid values are regular expressions. By default, each new line in the log files is parsed as one record.
skipHeaderLines	The number of lines for the agent to skip parsing at the beginning of monitored files. Value range: 0 or more Default: 0 (zero)
truncatedRecordTerminator	The string that the agent uses to truncate a parsed record when the record size exceeds the Kinesis Firehose record size limit. (1,000 KB) Default: '\n' (newline)

Monitor Multiple File Directories and Write to Multiple Streams

By specifying multiple flow configuration settings, you can configure the agent to monitor multiple file directories and send data to multiple streams. In the following configuration example, the agent monitors two file directories and sends data to an Kinesis stream and a Kinesis Firehose delivery stream respectively. Note that you can specify different endpoints for Kinesis Data Streams and Kinesis Firehose so that your Kinesis stream and Kinesis Firehose delivery stream don't need to be in the same region.

```
1  {
2      "cloudwatch.emitMetrics": true,
3      "kinesis.endpoint": "https://your/kinesis/endpoint",
4      "firehose.endpoint": "https://your/firehose/endpoint",
5      "flows": [
6          {
7              "filePattern": "/tmp/app1.log*",
8              "kinesisStream": "yourkinesisstream"
9          },
10          {
11              "filePattern": "/tmp/app2.log*",
12              "deliveryStream": "yourfirehosedeliverystream"
13          }
14      ]
15  }
```

For more detailed information about using the agent with Amazon Kinesis Data Streams, see Writing to Amazon Kinesis Data Streams with Kinesis Agent.

Use the Agent to Pre-process Data

The agent can pre-process the records parsed from monitored files before sending them to your delivery stream. You can enable this feature by adding the `dataProcessingOptions` configuration setting to your file flow. One or more processing options can be added and they will be performed in the specified order.

The agent supports the following processing options. Because the agent is open-source, you can further develop and extend its processing options. You can download the agent from Kinesis Agent.Processing Options

SINGLELINE
Converts a multi-line record to a single line record by removing newline characters, leading spaces, and trailing spaces.

```
1  {
2      "optionName": "SINGLELINE"
3  }
```

CSVTOJSON
Converts a record from delimiter separated format to JSON format.

```
1  {
2      "optionName": "CSVTOJSON",
3      "customFieldNames": [ "field1", "field2", ... ],
4      "delimiter": "yourdelimiter"
5  }
```

customFieldNames
[Required] The field names used as keys in each JSON key value pair. For example, if you specify ["f1", "f2"], the record "v1, v2" is converted to {"f1":"v1","f2":"v2"}.
delimiter
The string used as the delimiter in the record. The default is a comma (,).

LOGTOJSON
Converts a record from a log format to JSON format. The supported log formats are Apache Common Log, Apache Combined Log, Apache Error Log, and RFC3164 Syslog.

```
1  {
2      "optionName": "LOGTOJSON",
```

26

```
3        "logFormat": "logformat",
4        "matchPattern": "yourregexpattern",
5        "customFieldNames": [ "field1", "field2", … ]
6  }
```

logFormat

[Required] The log entry format. The following are possible values:

- COMMONAPACHELOG — The Apache Common Log format. Each log entry has the following pattern by default: "%{host} %{ident} %{authuser} [%{datetime}] \"%{request}\" %{response} %{bytes}".
- COMBINEDAPACHELOG — The Apache Combined Log format. Each log entry has the following pattern by default: "%{host} %{ident} %{authuser} [%{datetime}] \"%{request}\" %{response} %{bytes} %{referrer} %{agent}".
- APACHEERRORLOG — The Apache Error Log format. Each log entry has the following pattern by default: "[%{timestamp}] [%{module}:%{severity}] [pid %{processid}:tid %{threadid}] [client : %{client}] %{message}".
- SYSLOG — The RFC3164 Syslog format. Each log entry has the following pattern by default: "%{timestamp} %{hostname} %{program}[%{processid}]: %{message}".
  matchPattern
  Overrides the default pattern for the specified log format. Use this setting to extract values from log entries if they use a custom format. If you specify matchPattern, you must also specify customFieldNames.
  customFieldNames
  The custom field names used as keys in each JSON key value pair. You can use this setting to define field names for values extracted from matchPattern, or override the default field names of predefined log formats.

Example : LOGTOJSON Configuration Here is one example of a LOGTOJSON configuration for an Apache Common Log entry converted to JSON format:

```
1  {
2        "optionName": "LOGTOJSON",
3        "logFormat": "COMMONAPACHELOG"
4  }
```

Before conversion:

```
1  64.242.88.10 - - [07/Mar/2004:16:10:02 -0800] "GET /mailman/listinfo/hsdivision HTTP/1.1" 200
      6291
```

After conversion:

```
1  {"host":"64.242.88.10","ident":null,"authuser":null,"datetime":"07/Mar/2004:16:10:02 -0800","
      request":"GET /mailman/listinfo/hsdivision HTTP/1.1","response":"200","bytes":"6291"}
```

Example : LOGTOJSON Configuration With Custom Fields Here is another example LOGTOJSON configuration:

```
1  {
2        "optionName": "LOGTOJSON",
3        "logFormat": "COMMONAPACHELOG",
4        "customFieldNames": ["f1", "f2", "f3", "f4", "f5", "f6", "f7"]
5  }
```

With this configuration setting, the same Apache Common Log entry from the previous example is converted to JSON format as follows:

```
1  {"f1":"64.242.88.10","f2":null,"f3":null,"f4":"07/Mar/2004:16:10:02 -0800","f5":"GET /mailman/
      listinfo/hsdivision HTTP/1.1","f6":"200","f7":"6291"}
```

Example : Convert Apache Common Log Entry The following flow configuration converts an Apache Common Log entry to a single line record in JSON format:

```
1  {
2      "flows": [
3          {
4              "filePattern": "/tmp/app.log*",
5              "deliveryStream": "my-delivery-stream",
6              "dataProcessingOptions": [
7                  {
8                      "optionName": "LOGTOJSON",
9                      "logFormat": "COMMONAPACHELOG"
10                 }
11             ]
12         }
13     ]
14 }
```

Example : Convert Multi-Line Records The following flow configuration parses multi-line records whose first line starts with "[SEQUENCE=". Each record is first converted to a single line record. Then, values are extracted from the record based on a tab delimiter. Extracted values are mapped to specified customFieldNames values to form a single-line record in JSON format.

```
1  {
2      "flows": [
3          {
4              "filePattern": "/tmp/app.log*",
5              "deliveryStream": "my-delivery-stream",
6              "multiLineStartPattern": "\\[SEQUENCE=",
7              "dataProcessingOptions": [
8                  {
9                      "optionName": "SINGLELINE"
10                 },
11                 {
12                     "optionName": "CSVTOJSON",
13                     "customFieldNames": [ "field1", "field2", "field3" ],
14                     "delimiter": "\\t"
15                 }
16             ]
17         }
18     ]
19 }
```

Example : LOGTOJSON Configuration with Match Pattern Here is one example of a LOGTOJSON configuration for an Apache Common Log entry converted to JSON format, with the last field (bytes) omitted:

```
1  {
2      "optionName": "LOGTOJSON",
3      "logFormat": "COMMONAPACHELOG",
4      "matchPattern": "^([\\d.]+) (\\S+) (\\S+) \\[([\\w:/]+\\s[+\\-]\\d{4})\\] \"(.+?)\" (\\d{3})
        ",
5      "customFieldNames": ["host", "ident", "authuser", "datetime", "request", "response"]
6  }
```

Before conversion:

```
1  123.45.67.89 - - [27/Oct/2000:09:27:09 -0400] "GET /java/javaResources.html HTTP/1.0" 200
```

After conversion:

```
1 {"host":"123.45.67.89","ident":null,"authuser":null,"datetime":"27/Oct/2000:09:27:09 -0400","
    request":"GET /java/javaResources.html HTTP/1.0","response":"200"}
```

Agent CLI Commands

Automatically start the agent on system startup:

```
1 sudo chkconfig aws-kinesis-agent on
```

Check the status of the agent:

```
1 sudo service aws-kinesis-agent status
```

Stop the agent:

```
1 sudo service aws-kinesis-agent stop
```

Read the agent's log file from this location:

```
1 /var/log/aws-kinesis-agent/aws-kinesis-agent.log
```

Uninstall the agent:

```
1 sudo yum remove aws-kinesis-agent
```

Writing to a Kinesis Data Delivery Stream Using the AWS SDK

You can use the Kinesis Data Firehose API to send data to a Kinesis data delivery stream using the AWS SDK for Java, .NET, Node.js, Python, or Ruby. If you are new to Kinesis Data Firehose, take some time to become familiar with the concepts and terminology presented in What Is Amazon Kinesis Data Firehose?. For more information, see Start Developing with Amazon Web Services.

These examples do not represent production-ready code, in that they do not check for all possible exceptions, or account for all possible security or performance considerations.

The Kinesis Data Firehose API offers two operations for sending data to your Kinesis data delivery stream: PutRecord and PutRecordBatch. `PutRecord()` sends one data record within one call and `PutRecordBatch()` can send multiple data records within one call.

Topics

- Single Write Operations Using PutRecord
- Batch Write Operations Using PutRecordBatch

Single Write Operations Using PutRecord

Putting data requires only the Kinesis data delivery stream name and a byte buffer (<=1000 KB). Because Kinesis Data Firehose batches multiple records before loading the file into Amazon S3, you may want to add a record separator. To put data one record at a time into a Kinesis data delivery stream, use the following code:

```
1 PutRecordRequest putRecordRequest = new PutRecordRequest();
2 putRecordRequest.setDeliveryStreamName(deliveryStreamName);
3
4 String data = line + "\n";
5
6 Record record = createRecord(data);
7 putRecordRequest.setRecord(record);
8
9 // Put record into the DeliveryStream
10 firehoseClient.putRecord(putRecordRequest);
```

For more code context, see the sample code included in the AWS SDK. For information about request and response syntax, see the relevant topic in Amazon Kinesis Firehose API Operations.

Batch Write Operations Using PutRecordBatch

Putting data requires only the Kinesis data delivery stream name and a list of records. Because Kinesis Data Firehose batches multiple records before loading the file into Amazon S3, you may want to add a record separator. To put data records in batches into a Kinesis data delivery stream, use the following code:

```
1 PutRecordBatchRequest putRecordBatchRequest = new PutRecordBatchRequest();
2 putRecordBatchRequest.setDeliveryStreamName(deliveryStreamName);
3 putRecordBatchRequest.setRecords(recordList);
4
5 // Put Record Batch records. Max No.Of Records we can put in a
6 // single put record batch request is 500
7 firehoseClient.putRecordBatch(putRecordBatchRequest);
8
9 recordList.clear();
```

For more code context, see the sample code included in the AWS SDK. For information about request and response syntax, see the relevant topic in Amazon Kinesis Firehose API Operations.

Writing to Amazon Kinesis Data Firehose Using CloudWatch Logs

For information on how to create a CloudWatch Logs subscription that sends log events to Kinesis Data Firehose, see Subscription Filters with Amazon Kinesis Firehose.

Writing to Amazon Kinesis Data Firehose Using CloudWatch Events

You can configure Amazon CloudWatch to send events to a Kinesis Data Firehose delivery stream by adding a target to a CloudWatch Events rule.

To create a target for a CloudWatch Events rule that sends events to an existing Kinesis Data Firehose delivery stream

1. When creating your rule, in the **Step 1: Create Rule** page, for Targets, choose Add target, and then choose **Firehose delivery stream**.

2. For Delivery stream, select an existing Kinesis Data Firehose delivery stream.

For more information on creating CloudWatch Events rules, see Getting Started with Amazon CloudWatch Events.

Writing to Amazon Kinesis Data Firehose Using AWS IoT

You can configure AWS IoT to send information to a Kinesis Data Firehose delivery stream by adding an action.

To create an action that sends events to an existing Kinesis Data Firehose delivery stream

1. When creating your rule, in the **Set one or more actions** page, choose Add action, and then choose **Send messages to an Amazon Kinesis Data Firehose stream**.

2. Choose **Configure action**.

3. For **Stream name**, select an existing Kinesis Data Firehose delivery stream.

4. For **Separator**, choose a separator character to be inserted between records.

5. For **IAM role name**, choose an existing IAM role or choose **Create a new role**.

6. Choose **Add action**.

For more information on creating AWS IoT rules, see AWS IoT Rule Tutorials.

Amazon Kinesis Data Firehose Data Transformation

Kinesis Data Firehose can invoke your Lambda function to transform incoming source data and deliver the transformed data to destinations. You can enable Kinesis Data Firehose data transformation when you create your delivery stream.

Data Transformation Flow

When you enable Kinesis Data Firehose data transformation, Kinesis Data Firehose buffers incoming data up to 3 MB by default. (To adjust the buffering size, use the ProcessingConfiguration API with the ProcessorParameter called `BufferSizeInMBs`.) Kinesis Data Firehose then invokes the specified Lambda function asynchronously with each buffered batch using the AWS Lambda synchronous invocation mode. The transformed data is sent from Lambda to Kinesis Data Firehose, which then sends it to the destination when the specified destination buffering size or buffering interval is reached, whichever happens first.

Important
The Lambda synchronous invocation mode has a payload size limit of 6 MB for both the request and the response. Make sure that your buffering size for sending the request to the function is less than or equal to 6 MB and that the response returned by your function doesn't exceed 6 MB, either.

Data Transformation and Status Model

All transformed records from Lambda must contain the following parameters or Kinesis Data Firehose rejects them and treats that as a data transformation failure.

recordId
The record ID is passed from Kinesis Data Firehose to Lambda during the invocation. The transformed record must contain the same record ID. Any mismatch between the ID of the original record and the ID of the transformed record is treated as a data transformation failure.

result
The status of the data transformation of the record. The possible values are: "Ok" (the record was transformed successfully), "Dropped" (the record was dropped intentionally by your processing logic), and "ProcessingFailed" (the record could not be transformed). If a record has a status of "Ok" or "Dropped", Kinesis Data Firehose considers it successfully processed. Otherwise, Kinesis Data Firehose considers it unsuccessfully processed.

data
The transformed data payload, after base64-encoding.

Lambda Blueprints

Kinesis Data Firehose provides the following Lambda blueprints that you can use to create a Lambda function for data transformation.

- **General Firehose Processing** — Contains the data transformation and status model described in the previous section. Use this blueprint for any custom transformation logic.
- **Apache Log to JSON** — Parses and converts Apache log lines to JSON objects, using predefined JSON field names.
- **Apache Log to CSV** — Parses and converts Apache log lines to CSV format.
- **Syslog to JSON** — Parses and converts Syslog lines to JSON objects, using predefined JSON field names.
- **Syslog to CSV** — Parses and converts Syslog lines to CSV format.
- **Kinesis Firehose Process Record Streams as source** — Accesses the Kinesis Data Streams records in the input and returns them with a processing status.

- **Kinesis Firehose CloudWatch Logs Processor** — Parses and extracts individual log events from records sent by CloudWatch Logs subscription filters.

Note

Lambda blueprints are only available in the Node.js and Python languages. You can implement your own functions in other supported languages. For information on AWS Lambda supported languages, see Introduction: Building Lambda Functions.

Data Transformation Failure Handling

If your Lambda function invocation fails because of a network timeout or because you've reached the Lambda invocation limit, Kinesis Data Firehose retries the invocation three times by default. If the invocation does not succeed, Kinesis Data Firehose then skips that batch of records. The skipped records are treated as unsuccessfully processed records. You can specify or override the retry options using the CreateDeliveryStream or UpdateDestination API. For this type of failure, you can log invocation errors to Amazon CloudWatch Logs. For more information, see Monitoring with Amazon CloudWatch Logs.

If the status of the data transformation of a record is `ProcessingFailed`, Kinesis Data Firehose treats the record as unsuccessfully processed. For this type of failure, you can emit error logs to Amazon CloudWatch Logs from your Lambda function. For more information, see Accessing Amazon CloudWatch Logs for AWS Lambda in the *AWS Lambda Developer Guide*.

If data transformation fails, the unsuccessfully processed records are delivered to your S3 bucket in the `processing_failed` folder. The records have the following format:

```
1  {
2      "attemptsMade": "count",
3      "arrivalTimestamp": "timestamp",
4      "errorCode": "code",
5      "errorMessage": "message",
6      "attemptEndingTimestamp": "timestamp",
7      "rawData": "data",
8      "lambdaArn": "arn"
9  }
```

`attemptsMade`
The number of invocation requests attempted.

`arrivalTimestamp`
The time that the record was received by Kinesis Data Firehose.

`errorCode`
The HTTP error code returned by Lambda.

`errorMessage`
The error message returned by Lambda.

`attemptEndingTimestamp`
The time that Kinesis Data Firehose stopped attempting Lambda invocations.

`rawData`
The base64-encoded record data.

`lambdaArn`
The Amazon Resource Name (ARN) of the Lambda function.

Source Record Backup

Kinesis Data Firehose can back up all untransformed records to your S3 bucket concurrently while delivering transformed records to the destination. You can enable source record backup when you create or update your delivery stream. You cannot disable source record backup after you enable it.

Converting Your Input Record Format in Kinesis Data Firehose

Amazon Kinesis Data Firehose can convert the format of your input data from JSON to Apache Parquet or Apache ORC before storing the data in Amazon S3. Parquet and ORC are columnar data formats that save space and enable faster queries compared to row-oriented formats like JSON. If you want to convert an input format other than JSON, such as comma-separated values (CSV) or structured text, you can use AWS Lambda to transform it to JSON first. For more information, see Amazon Kinesis Data Firehose Data Transformation.

Topics

- Record Format Conversion Requirements
- Choosing the JSON Deserializer
- Choosing the Serializer
- Converting Input Record Format (Console)
- Converting Input Record Format (API)
- Record Format Conversion Error Handling

Record Format Conversion Requirements

Kinesis Data Firehose requires the following three elements to convert the format of your record data:

- **A deserializer to read the JSON of your input data** – You can choose one of two types of deserializers: Apache Hive JSON SerDe or OpenX JSON SerDe.
- **A schema to determine how to interpret that data** – Use AWS Glue to create a schema in the AWS Glue Data Catalog. Kinesis Data Firehose then references that schema and uses it to interpret your input data. You can use the same schema to configure both Kinesis Data Firehose and your analytics software. For more information, see Populating the AWS Glue Data Catalog in the *AWS Glue Developer Guide*.
- **A serializer to convert the data to the target columnar storage format (Parquet or ORC)** – You can choose one of two types of serializers: ORC SerDe or Parquet SerDe.

Important

If you enable record format conversion, you can't set your Kinesis Data Firehose destination to be Amazon Elasticsearch Service (Amazon ES), Amazon Redshift, or Splunk. With format conversion enabled, Amazon S3 is the only destination that you can use for your Kinesis Data Firehose delivery stream.

You can convert the format of your data even if you aggregate your records before sending them to Kinesis Data Firehose.

Choosing the JSON Deserializer

Choose the OpenX JSON SerDe if your input JSON contains time stamps in the following formats:

- yyyy-MM-dd'T'HH:mm:ss'Z' – For example, `2017-02-07T15:13:01Z`. However, milliseconds aren't supported.
- yyyy-MM-dd HH:mm:ss – For example, `2017-02-07 15:13:01`. However, milliseconds aren't supported.
- Epoch seconds – For example, `1518033528`.
- Epoch milliseconds – For example, `1518033528123`.
- Floating point epoch seconds – For example, `1518033528.123`.

The OpenX JSON SerDe can convert periods (.) to underscores (_). It can also convert JSON keys to lowercase before deserializing them. For more information about the options that are available with this deserializer through Kinesis Data Firehose, see OpenXJsonSerDe.

If you're not sure which deserializer to choose, use the OpenX JSON SerDe, unless you have time stamps that it doesn't support.

If you have time stamps in formats other than those listed previously, use the Apache Hive JSON SerDe. When you choose this deserializer, you can specify the time stamp formats to use. To do this, follow the pattern syntax of the Joda-Time `DateTimeFormat` format strings. For more information, see Class DateTimeFormat.

You can also use the special value `millis` to parse time stamps in epoch milliseconds. If you don't specify a format, Kinesis Data Firehose uses `java.sql.Timestamp::valueOf` by default.

The Hive JSON SerDe doesn't allow the following:

- Periods (`.`) in column names.
- Fields whose type is `uniontype`.
- Fields that have numerical types in the schema, but that are strings in the JSON. For example, if the schema is (an int), and the JSON is `{"a":"123"}`, the Hive SerDe gives an error.

The Hive SerDe doesn't convert nested JSON into strings. For example, if you have `{"a":{"inner":1}}`, it doesn't treat `{"inner":1}` as a string.

Choosing the Serializer

The serializer that you choose depends on your business needs. To learn more about the two serializer options, see ORC SerDe and Parquet SerDe.

Converting Input Record Format (Console)

You can enable data format conversion on the console when you create or update a Kinesis delivery stream. With data format conversion enabled, Amazon S3 is the only destination that you can configure for the delivery stream. Also, Amazon S3 compression gets disabled when you enable format conversion. However, Snappy compression happens automatically as part of the conversion process.

To enable data format conversion for a data delivery stream

1. Sign in to the AWS Management Console, and open the Kinesis Data Firehose console at https://console.aws.amazon.com/firehose/.

2. Choose a Kinesis Data Firehose delivery stream to update, or create a new delivery stream by following the steps in Creating an Amazon Kinesis Data Firehose Delivery Stream.

3. Under **Convert record format**, set **Record format conversion** to **Enabled**.

4. Choose the output format that you want. For more information about the two options, see Apache Parquet and Apache ORC.

5. Choose an AWS Glue table to specify a schema for your source records. Set the Region, database, table, and table version.

Converting Input Record Format (API)

If you want Kinesis Data Firehose to convert the format of your input data from JSON to Parquet or ORC, specify the optional DataFormatConversionConfiguration element in ExtendedS3DestinationConfiguration or in ExtendedS3DestinationUpdate. If you specify DataFormatConversionConfiguration, the following restrictions apply:

- In BufferingHints, you can't set `SizeInMBs` to a value less than 64 if you enable record format conversion. Also, when format conversion isn't enabled, the default value is 5. The value becomes 128 when you enable it.

- You must set `CompressionFormat` in ExtendedS3DestinationConfiguration or in ExtendedS3DestinationUpdate to `UNCOMPRESSED`. The default value for `CompressionFormat` is `UNCOMPRESSED`. Therefore, you can also leave it unspecified in ExtendedS3DestinationConfiguration. The data still gets compressed as part of the serialization process, using Snappy compression by default. When you configure the serializer, you can choose other types of compression.

Record Format Conversion Error Handling

When Kinesis Data Firehose can't parse or deserialize a record (for example, when the data doesn't match the schema), it writes it to Amazon S3 with an error prefix. If this write fails, Kinesis Data Firehose retries it forever, blocking further delivery. For each failed record, Kinesis Data Firehose writes a JSON document with the following schema:

```
1  {
2    "attemptsMade": long,
3    "arrivalTimestamp": long,
4    "lastErrorCode": string,
5    "lastErrorMessage": string,
6    "attemptEndingTimestamp": long,
7    "rawData": string,
8    "sequenceNumber": string,
9    "subSequenceNumber": long,
10   "dataCatalogTable": {
11     "catalogId": string,
12     "databaseName": string,
13     "tableName": string,
14     "region": string,
15     "versionId": string,
16     "catalogArn": string
17   }
18 }
```

Amazon Kinesis Data Firehose Data Delivery

After data is sent to your delivery stream, it is automatically delivered to the destination you choose.

Topics

- Data Delivery Format
- Data Delivery Frequency
- Data Delivery Failure Handling
- Amazon S3 Object Name Format
- Index Rotation for the Amazon ES Destination

Data Delivery Format

For data delivery to Amazon S3, Kinesis Firehose concatenates multiple incoming records based on buffering configuration of your delivery stream, and then delivers them to Amazon S3 as an S3 object. You may want to add a record separator at the end of each record before you send it to Kinesis Firehose so that you can divide a delivered S3 object to individual records.

For data delivery to Amazon Redshift, Kinesis Firehose first delivers incoming data to your S3 bucket in the format described earlier. Kinesis Firehose then issues an Amazon Redshift COPY command to load the data from your S3 bucket to your Amazon Redshift cluster. You need to make sure that after Kinesis Firehose concatenates multiple incoming records to an S3 object, the S3 object can be copied to your Amazon Redshift cluster. For more information, see Amazon Redshift COPY Command Data Format Parameters.

For data delivery to Amazon ES, Kinesis Firehose buffers incoming records based on buffering configuration of your delivery stream. It then generates an Elasticsearch bulk request to index multiple records to your Elasticsearch cluster. You need to make sure that your record is UTF-8 encoded and flattened to a single-line JSON object before you send it to Kinesis Firehose. Also, the `rest.action.multi.allow_explicit_index` option for your Elasticsearch cluster must be set to true (default) in order to take bulk requests with an explicit index that is set per record. For more information, see Amazon ES Configure Advanced Options in the *Amazon Elasticsearch Service Developer Guide*.

For data delivery to Splunk, Kinesis Data Firehose concatenates the bytes that you send. If you want delimiters in your data, such as a new line character, you must insert them yourself. Make sure that Splunk is configured to parse any such delimiters.

Data Delivery Frequency

Each Kinesis Data Firehose destination has its own data delivery frequency.

Amazon S3

The frequency of data delivery to Amazon S3 is determined by the S3 **Buffer size** and **Buffer interval** value you configured for your delivery stream. Kinesis Data Firehose buffers incoming data before delivering it to Amazon S3. You can configure the values for S3 **Buffer size** (1–128 MB) or **Buffer interval** (60–900 seconds), and the condition satisfied first triggers data delivery to Amazon S3. In circumstances where data delivery to the destination is falling behind data writing to the delivery stream, Kinesis Data Firehose raises the buffer size dynamically to catch up and make sure that all data is delivered to the destination.

Amazon Redshift

The frequency of data COPY operations from Amazon S3 to Amazon Redshift is determined by how fast your Amazon Redshift cluster can finish the COPY command. If there is still data to copy, Kinesis Data Firehose issues a new COPY command as soon as the previous COPY command is successfully finished by Amazon Redshift.

Amazon Elasticsearch Service

The frequency of data delivery to Amazon ES is determined by the Elasticsearch **Buffer size** and **Buffer interval** values that you configured for your delivery stream. Kinesis Data Firehose buffers incoming data before delivering it to Amazon ES. You can configure the values for Elasticsearch **Buffer size** (1–100 MB) or **Buffer interval** (60–900 seconds), and the condition satisfied first triggers data delivery to Amazon ES.

Splunk

Kinesis Data Firehose buffers incoming data before delivering it to Splunk. The buffer size is 5 MB and the buffer interval is 60 seconds. The condition satisfied first triggers data delivery to Splunk. The buffer size and interval aren't configurable. These numbers are optimal.

Data Delivery Failure Handling

Each Kinesis Data Firehose destination has its own data delivery failure handling.

Amazon S3

Data delivery to your S3 bucket might fail for reasons such as the bucket doesn't exist anymore, the IAM role that Kinesis Firehose assumes doesn't have access to the bucket, the network failed, or similar events. Under these conditions, Kinesis Firehose keeps retrying for up to 24 hours until the delivery succeeds. The maximum data storage time of Kinesis Firehose is 24 hours, and your data is lost if data delivery fails for more than 24 hours.

Amazon Redshift

For the Amazon Redshift destination, you can specify a retry duration (0–7200 seconds) when creating a delivery stream.
Data delivery to your Amazon Redshift cluster might fail for reasons such as an incorrect Amazon Redshift cluster configuration of your delivery stream, an Amazon Redshift cluster under maintenance, network failure, or similar events. Under these conditions, Kinesis Data Firehose retries for the specified time duration and skips that particular batch of S3 objects. The skipped objects' information is delivered to your S3 bucket as a manifest file in the `errors/` folder, which you can use for manual backfill. For information about how to COPY data manually with manifest files, see Using a Manifest to Specify Data Files.

Amazon Elasticsearch Service

For the Amazon ES destination, you can specify a retry duration (0–7200 seconds) when creating a delivery stream.
Data delivery to your Amazon ES cluster might fail for reasons such as an incorrect Amazon ES cluster configuration of your delivery stream, an Amazon ES cluster under maintenance, network failure, or similar events. Under these conditions, Kinesis Data Firehose retries for the specified time duration and then skips that particular index request. The skipped documents are delivered to your S3 bucket in the `elasticsearch_failed/` folder, which you can use for manual backfill. Each document has the following JSON format:

```
1  {
2      "attemptsMade": "(number of index requests attempted)",
3      "arrivalTimestamp": "(the time when the document was received by Firehose)",
4      "errorCode": "(http error code returned by Elasticsearch)",
5      "errorMessage": "(error message returned by Elasticsearch)",
6      "attemptEndingTimestamp": "(the time when Firehose stopped attempting index request)",
7      "esDocumentId": "(intended Elasticsearch document ID)",
8      "esIndexName": "(intended Elasticsearch index name)",
9      "esTypeName": "(intended Elasticsearch type name)",
10     "rawData": "(base64-encoded document data)"
11 }
```

Splunk

When Kinesis Data Firehose sends data to Splunk, it waits for acknowledgment from Splunk. If an error occurs or the acknowledgment doesn't arrive within the acknowledgment timeout period, Kinesis Firehose starts the retry duration counter and keeps retrying until the retry duration expires, after which Kinesis Firehose considers it a data delivery failure and backs up the data to your Amazon S3 bucket.

Every time Kinesis Firehose sends data to Splunk, whether it's the initial attempt or a retry, it restarts the acknowledgement timeout counter and waits for an acknowledgement to arrive from Splunk. Even if the retry duration expires, Kinesis Firehose still waits for the acknowledgment until it receives it or the acknowledgement timeout is reached. If the acknowledgment times out, Kinesis Firehose checks to determine whether there's time left in the retry counter. If there is time left, it retries again and repeats the logic until it receives an acknowledgment or determines that the retry time has expired.

A failure to receive an acknowledgement isn't the only kind of data delivery error that can occur. For information about the other types of data delivery errors that you might encounter, see Splunk Data Delivery Errors. Any data delivery error triggers the retry logic if your retry duration is greater than 0.

The following is an example error record.

```
1  {
2    "attemptsMade": 0,
3    "arrivalTimestamp": 1506035354675,
4    "errorCode": "Splunk.AckTimeout",
5    "errorMessage": "Did not receive an acknowledgement from HEC before the HEC acknowledgement
          timeout expired. Despite the acknowledgement timeout, it's possible the data was indexed
          successfully in Splunk. Kinesis Firehose backs up in Amazon S3 data for which the
          acknowledgement timeout expired.",
6    "attemptEndingTimestamp": 13626284715507,
7    "rawData": "
          MiAyNTE2MjAyNzIyMDkgZW5pLTA1ZjMyMmQ1IDIxOC45Mi4xODguMjE0IDE3Mi4xNi4xLjE2NyAyNTIzMyAxNDMzIDYgMSA
          ==",
8    "EventId": "49577193928114147339600778471082492393164139877200035842.0"
9  }
```

Amazon S3 Object Name Format

Kinesis Data Firehose adds a UTC time prefix in the format YYYY/MM/DD/HH before writing objects to Amazon S3. This prefix creates a logical hierarchy in the bucket, where each forward slash (/) creates a level in the hierarchy. You can modify this structure by adding to the start of the prefix when you create the Kinesis data delivery stream. For example, add myApp/ to use the myApp/YYYY/MM/DD/HH prefix or myApp to use the myApp YYYY/MM/DD/HH prefix.

The S3 object name follows the pattern DeliveryStreamName-DeliveryStreamVersion-YYYY-MM-DD-HH-MM-SS-RandomString, where DeliveryStreamVersion begins with 1 and increases by 1 for every configuration change of the Kinesis data delivery stream. You can change Kinesis data delivery stream configurations (for example, the name of the S3 bucket, buffering hints, compression, and encryption) using the Kinesis Data Firehose console, or by using the UpdateDestination API operation.

Index Rotation for the Amazon ES Destination

For the Amazon ES destination, you can specify a time-based index rotation option from one of the following five options: NoRotation, OneHour, OneDay, OneWeek, or OneMonth.

Depending on the rotation option you choose, Kinesis Data Firehose appends a portion of the UTC arrival time stamp to your specified index name, and rotates the appended time stamp accordingly. The following example shows the resulting index name in Amazon ES for each index rotation option, where the specified index name is myindex and the arrival time stamp is 2016-02-25T13:00:00Z.

RotationPeriod	IndexName
NoRotation	myindex

RotationPeriod	IndexName
OneHour	myindex-2016-02-25-13
OneDay	myindex-2016-02-25
OneWeek	myindex-2016-w08
OneMonth	myindex-2016-02

Using Server-Side Encryption with Amazon Kinesis Data Firehose

If you have sensitive data, you can enable server-side data encryption when you use Amazon Kinesis Data Firehose. However, this is only possible if you use a Kinesis stream as your data source. When you configure a Kinesis stream as the data source of a Kinesis Data Firehose delivery stream, Kinesis Data Firehose no longer stores the data at rest. Instead, the data is stored in the Kinesis stream.

When you send data from your data producers to your Kinesis stream, the Kinesis Data Streams service encrypts your data using an AWS KMS key before storing it at rest. When your Kinesis Data Firehose delivery stream reads the data from your Kinesis stream, the Kinesis Data Streams service first decrypts the data and then sends it to Kinesis Data Firehose. Kinesis Data Firehose buffers the data in memory based on the buffering hints that you specify and then delivers it to your destinations without storing the unencrypted data at rest.

For information about how to enable server-side encryption for Kinesis Data Streams, see Using Server-Side Encryption.

Monitoring Amazon Kinesis Data Firehose

You can monitor Amazon Kinesis Data Firehose using the following features:

- CloudWatch metrics— Kinesis Data Firehose sends Amazon CloudWatch custom metrics with detailed monitoring for each delivery stream.
- CloudWatch Logs— Kinesis Data Firehose sends CloudWatch custom logs with detailed monitoring for each delivery stream.
- Kinesis Agent— Kinesis Agent publishes custom CloudWatch metrics to help assess whether the agent is working as expected.
- API logging and history— Kinesis Data Firehose uses AWS CloudTrail to log API calls and store the data in an Amazon S3 bucket, and to maintain API call history.

Monitoring with Amazon CloudWatch Metrics

Kinesis Data Firehose integrates with CloudWatch metrics so that you can collect, view, and analyze Cloud-Watch metrics for your Kinesis data delivery streams. For example, you can monitor the `IncomingBytes` and `IncomingRecords` metrics to keep track of data ingested into Kinesis Data Firehose from data producers.

The metrics that you configure for your Kinesis data delivery streams and agents are automatically collected and pushed to CloudWatch every five minutes. Metrics are archived for two weeks; after that period, the data is discarded.

The metrics collected for Kinesis data delivery streams are free of charge. For information about Kinesis agent metrics, see Monitoring Kinesis Agent Health.

Topics

- Service-level CloudWatch Metrics
- API-Level CloudWatch Metrics
- Data Transformation CloudWatch Metrics
- Format Conversion CloudWatch Metrics
- Dimensions for Kinesis Data Firehose
- Accessing CloudWatch Metrics for Kinesis Data Firehose

Service-level CloudWatch Metrics

The `AWS/Firehose` namespace includes the following service-level metrics.

Metric	Description
BackupToS3.Bytes	The number of bytes delivered to Amazon S3 for backup over the specified time period. Kinesis Data Firehose emits this metric when data transformation is enabled for Amazon S3 or Amazon Redshift destinations. Units: Bytes
BackupToS3.DataFreshness	Age (from getting into Kinesis Data Firehose to now) of the oldest record in Kinesis Data Firehose. Any record older than this age has been delivered to the Amazon S3 bucket for backup. Kinesis Data Firehose emits this metric when data transformation is enabled for Amazon S3 or Amazon Redshift destinations. Units: Seconds
BackupToS3.Records	The number of records delivered to Amazon S3 for backup over the specified time period. Kinesis Data Firehose emits this metric when data transformation is enabled for Amazon S3 or Amazon Redshift destinations. Units: Count
BackupToS3.Success	Sum of successful Amazon S3 put commands for backup over sum of all Amazon S3 backup put commands. Kinesis Data Firehose emits this metric when data transformation is enabled for Amazon S3 or Amazon Redshift destinations.
DeliveryToElasticsearch.Bytes	The number of bytes indexed to Amazon ES over the specified time period. Units: Bytes

Metric	Description
DeliveryToElasticsearch.Records	The number of records indexed to Amazon ES over the specified time period. Units: Count
DeliveryToElasticsearch.Success	The sum of the successfully indexed records over the sum of records that were attempted.
DeliveryToRedshift.Bytes	The number of bytes copied to Amazon Redshift over the specified time period. Units: Bytes
DeliveryToRedshift.Records	The number of records copied to Amazon Redshift over the specified time period. Units: Count
DeliveryToRedshift.Success	The sum of successful Amazon Redshift COPY commands over the sum of all Amazon Redshift COPY commands.
DeliveryToS3.Bytes	The number of bytes delivered to Amazon S3 over the specified time period. Units: Bytes
DeliveryToS3.DataFreshness	The age (from getting into Kinesis Data Firehose to now) of the oldest record in Kinesis Data Firehose. Any record older than this age has been delivered to the S3 bucket. Units: Seconds
DeliveryToS3.Records	The number of records delivered to Amazon S3 over the specified time period. Units: Count
DeliveryToS3.Success	The sum of successful Amazon S3 put commands over the sum of all Amazon S3 put commands.
DeliveryToSplunk.Bytes	The number of bytes delivered to Splunk over the specified time period. Units: Bytes
DeliveryToSplunk.DataFreshness	Age (from getting into Kinesis Firehose to now) of the oldest record in Kinesis Firehose. Any record older than this age has been delivered to Splunk. Units: Seconds
DeliveryToSplunk.Records	The number of records delivered to Splunk over the specified time period. Units: Count
DeliveryToSplunk.Success	The sum of the successfully indexed records over the sum of records that were attempted.
IncomingBytes	The number of bytes ingested into the Kinesis Data Firehose stream over the specified time period. Units: Bytes
IncomingRecords	The number of records ingested into the Kinesis Data Firehose stream over the specified time period. Units: Count

API-Level CloudWatch Metrics

The `AWS/Firehose` namespace includes the following API-level metrics.

Metric	Description

Metric	Description

Metric	Description
DescribeDeliveryStream.Latency	The time taken per `DescribeDeliveryStream` operation, measured over the specified time period. Units: Milliseconds
DescribeDeliveryStream.Requests	The total number of `DescribeDeliveryStream` requests. Units: Count
ListDeliveryStreams.Latency	The time taken per `ListDeliveryStream` operation, measured over the specified time period. Units: Milliseconds
ListDeliveryStreams.Requests	The total number of `ListFirehose` requests. Units: Count
PutRecord.Bytes	The number of bytes put to the Kinesis Data Firehose delivery stream using `PutRecord` over the specified time period. Units: Bytes
PutRecord.Latency	The time taken per `PutRecord` operation, measured over the specified time period. Units: Milliseconds
PutRecord.Requests	The total number of `PutRecord` requests, which is equal to total number of records from `PutRecord` operations. Units: Count
PutRecordBatch.Bytes	The number of bytes put to the Kinesis Data Firehose delivery stream using `PutRecordBatch` over the specified time period. Units: Bytes
PutRecordBatch.Latency	The time taken per `PutRecordBatch` operation, measured over the specified time period. Units: Milliseconds
PutRecordBatch.Records	The total number of records from `PutRecordBatch` operations. Units: Count
PutRecordBatch.Requests	The total number of `PutRecordBatch` requests. Units: Count
UpdateDeliveryStream.Latency	The time taken per `UpdateDeliveryStream` operation, measured over the specified time period. Units: Milliseconds
UpdateDeliveryStream.Requests	The total number of `UpdateDeliveryStream` requests. Units: Count

Data Transformation CloudWatch Metrics

If data transformation with Lambda is enabled, the `AWS/Firehose` namespace includes the following metrics.

Metric	Description
ExecuteProcessing.Duration	The time it takes for each Lambda function invocation performed by Kinesis Data Firehose. Units: Seconds
ExecuteProcessing.Success	The sum of the successful Lambda function invocations over the sum of the total Lambda function invocations.

Metric	Description
SucceedProcessing.Records	The number of successfully processed records over the specified time period. Units: Count
SucceedProcessing.Bytes	The number of successfully processed bytes over the specified time period. Units: Bytes

Format Conversion CloudWatch Metrics

If format conversion is enabled, the `AWS/Firehose` namespace includes the following metrics.

Metric	Description
SucceedConversion.Records	The number of successfully converted records. Units: Count
SucceedConversion.Bytes	The size of the successfully converted records. Units: Bytes
FailedConversion.Records	The number of records that could not be converted. Units: Count
FailedConversion.Bytes	The size of the records that could not be converted. Units: Bytes

Dimensions for Kinesis Data Firehose

To filter metrics by delivery stream, use the `DeliveryStreamName` dimension.

Accessing CloudWatch Metrics for Kinesis Data Firehose

You can monitor metrics for Kinesis Data Firehose using the CloudWatch console, command line, or CloudWatch API. The following procedures show you how to access metrics using these different methods.

To access metrics using the CloudWatch console

1. Open the CloudWatch console at https://console.aws.amazon.com/cloudwatch/.

2. On the navigation bar, choose a region.

3. In the navigation pane, choose **Metrics**.

4. Choose the **Firehose** namespace.

5. Choose **Delivery Stream Metrics** or **Firehose Metrics**.

6. Select a metric to add to the graph.

To access metrics using the AWS CLI
Use the list-metrics and get-metric-statistics commands.

```
1 aws cloudwatch list-metrics --namespace "AWS/Firehose"
```

```
1 aws cloudwatch get-metric-statistics --namespace "AWS/Firehose" \
2 --metric-name DescribeDeliveryStream.Latency --statistics Average --period 3600 \
3 --start-time 2017-06-01T00:00:00Z --endtime 2017-06-30T00:00:00Z
```

Monitoring with Amazon CloudWatch Logs

Kinesis Data Firehose integrates with CloudWatch Logs so that you can view the specific error logs when the Lambda invocation for data transformation or data delivery fails. You can enable Kinesis Data Firehose error logging when you create your delivery stream.

If you enable Kinesis Data Firehose error logging in the Kinesis Data Firehose console, a log group and corresponding log streams are created for the delivery stream on your behalf. The format of the log group name is `/aws/kinesisfirehose/delivery-stream-name`, where `delivery-stream-name` is the name of the corresponding delivery stream. The log stream name is **S3Delivery**, **RedshiftDelivery**, or **ElasticsearchDelivery**, depending on the delivery destination. Lambda invocation errors for data transformation are also logged to the log stream used for data delivery errors.

For example, if you create a delivery stream "MyStream" with Amazon Redshift as the destination and enable Kinesis Data Firehose error logging, the following are created on your behalf: a log group named `aws/kinesisfirehose/MyStream` and two log streams named **S3Delivery** and **RedshiftDelivery**. In this example, the **S3Delivery** log stream is used for logging errors related to delivery failure to the intermediate S3 bucket, and the **RedshiftDelivery** log stream is used for logging errors related to Lambda invocation failure and delivery failure to your Amazon Redshift cluster.

If you enable Kinesis Data Firehose error logging through the AWS CLI or an AWS SDK using the `CloudWatchLoggingOptions` configuration, you must create a log group and a log stream in advance. We recommend reserving that log group and log stream for Kinesis Data Firehose error logging exclusively. Also ensure that the associated IAM policy has `"logs:putLogEvents"` permission. For more information, see Controlling Access with Amazon Kinesis Data Firehose .

Note that Kinesis Data Firehose does not guarantee that all delivery error logs are sent to CloudWatch Logs. In circumstances where delivery failure rate is high, Kinesis Data Firehose samples delivery error logs before sending them to CloudWatch Logs.

There is a nominal charge for error logs sent to CloudWatch Logs. For more information, see Amazon CloudWatch Pricing.

Topics

- Data Delivery Errors
- Lambda Invocation Errors
- Accessing CloudWatch Logs for Kinesis Data Firehose

Data Delivery Errors

The following is a list of data delivery error codes and messages for each Kinesis Data Firehose destination. Each error message also describes the proper action to take to fix the issue.

Topics

- Amazon S3 Data Delivery Errors
- Amazon Redshift Data Delivery Errors
- Splunk Data Delivery Errors
- Amazon Elasticsearch Service Data Delivery Errors

Amazon S3 Data Delivery Errors

Kinesis Data Firehose can send the following Amazon S3-related errors to CloudWatch Logs.

Error Code	Error Message and Information
S3.KMS.NotFoundException	"The provided AWS KMS key was not found. If you are using what you believe to be a valid AWS KMS key with the correct role, check if there is a problem with the account to which the AWS KMS key is attached."
S3.KMS.RequestLimitExceeded	"The KMS request per second limit was exceeded while attempting to encrypt S3 objects. Increase the request per second limit." For more information, see Limits in the *AWS Key Management Service Developer Guide*.
S3.AccessDenied	"Access was denied. Ensure that the trust policy for the provided IAM role allows Kinesis Data Firehose to assume the role, and the access policy allows access to the S3 bucket."
S3.AccountProblem	"There is a problem with your AWS account that prevents the operation from completing successfully. Contact AWS Support."
S3.AllAccessDisabled	"Access to the account provided has been disabled. Contact AWS Support."
S3.InvalidPayer	"Access to the account provided has been disabled. Contact AWS Support."
S3.NotSignedUp	"The account is not signed up for Amazon S3. Sign the account up or use a different account."
S3.NoSuchBucket	"The specified bucket does not exist. Create the bucket or use a different bucket that does exist."
S3.MethodNotAllowed	"The specified method is not allowed against this resource. Modify the bucket's policy to allow the correct Amazon S3 operation permissions."
InternalError	"An internal error occurred while attempting to deliver data. Delivery will be retried; if the error persists, then it will be reported to AWS for resolution."

Amazon Redshift Data Delivery Errors

Kinesis Data Firehose can send the following Amazon Redshift-related errors to CloudWatch Logs.

Error Code	Error Message and Information
Redshift.TableNotFound	"The table to which to load data was not found. Ensure that the specified table exists." The destination table in Amazon Redshift to which data should be copied from S3 was not found. Note that Kinesis Data Firehose does not create the Amazon Redshift table if it does not exist.
Redshift.SyntaxError	"The COPY command contains a syntax error. Retry the command."

Error Code	Error Message and Information
Redshift.AuthenticationFailed	"The provided user name and password failed authentication. Provide a valid user name and password."
Redshift.AccessDenied	"Access was denied. Ensure that the trust policy for the provided IAM role allows Kinesis Data Firehose to assume the role."
Redshift.S3BucketAccessDenied	"The COPY command was unable to access the S3 bucket. Ensure that the access policy for the provided IAM role allows access to the S3 bucket."
Redshift.DataLoadFailed	"Loading data into the table failed. Check STL_LOAD_ERRORS system table for details."
Redshift.ColumnNotFound	"A column in the COPY command does not exist in the table. Specify a valid column name."
Redshift.DatabaseNotFound	"The database specified in the Amazon Redshift destination configuration or JDBC URL was not found. Specify a valid database name."
Redshift.IncorrectCopyOptions	"Conflicting or redundant COPY options were provided. Some options are not compatible in certain combinations. Check the COPY command reference for more info." For more information, see the Amazon Redshift COPY command in the *Amazon Redshift Database Developer Guide*.
Redshift.MissingColumn	"There is a column defined in the table schema as NOT NULL without a DEFAULT value and not included in the column list. Exclude this column, ensure that the loaded data always provides a value for this column, or add a default value to the Amazon Redshift schema for this table."
Redshift.ConnectionFailed	"The connection to the specified Amazon Redshift cluster failed. Ensure that security settings allow Kinesis Data Firehose connections, that the cluster or database specified in the Amazon Redshift destination configuration or JDBC URL is correct, and that the cluster is available."
Redshift.ColumnMismatch	"The number of jsonpaths in the COPY command and the number of columns in the destination table should match. Retry the command."
Redshift.IncorrectOrMissingRegion	"Amazon Redshift attempted to use the wrong region endpoint for accessing the S3 bucket. Either specify a correct region value in the COPY command options or ensure that the S3 bucket is in the same region as the Amazon Redshift database."
Redshift.IncorrectJsonPathsFile	"The provided jsonpaths file is not in a supported JSON format. Retry the command."

Error Code	Error Message and Information
Redshift.MissingS3File	"One or more S3 files required by Amazon Redshift have been removed from the S3 bucket. Check the S3 bucket policies to remove any automatic deletion of S3 files."
Redshift.InsufficientPrivilege	"The user does not have permissions to load data into the table. Check the Amazon Redshift user permissions for the INSERT privilege."
Redshift.ReadOnlyCluster	"The query cannot be executed because the system is in resize mode. Try the query again later."
Redshift.DiskFull	"Data could not be loaded because the disk is full. Increase the capacity of the Amazon Redshift cluster or delete unused data to free disk space."
InternalError	"An internal error occurred while attempting to deliver data. Delivery will be retried; if the error persists, then it will be reported to AWS for resolution."

Splunk Data Delivery Errors

Kinesis Data Firehose can send the following Splunk-related errors to CloudWatch Logs.

Error Code	Error Message and Information
Splunk.ProxyWithoutStickySessions	"If you have a proxy (ELB or other) between Kinesis Data Firehose and the HEC node, you must enable sticky sessions to support HEC ACKs."
Splunk.DisabledToken	"The HEC token is disabled. Enable the token to allow data delivery to Splunk."
Splunk.InvalidToken	"The HEC token is invalid. Update Kinesis Data Firehose with a valid HEC token."
Splunk.InvalidDataFormat	"The data is not formatted correctly. To see how to properly format data for Raw or Event HEC endpoints, see Splunk Event Data."
Splunk.InvalidIndex	"The HEC token or input is configured with an invalid index. Check your index configuration and try again."
Splunk.ServerError	"Data delivery to Splunk failed due to a server error from the HEC node. Kinesis Data Firehose will retry sending the data if the retry duration in your Kinesis Data Firehose is greater than 0. If all the retries fail, Kinesis Data Firehose backs up the data to Amazon S3."
Splunk.DisabledAck	"Indexer acknowledgement is disabled for the HEC token. Enable indexer acknowledgement and try again. For more info, see Enable indexer acknowledgement."

Error Code	Error Message and Information
Splunk.AckTimeout	"Did not receive an acknowledgement from HEC before the HEC acknowledgement timeout expired. Despite the acknowledgement timeout, it's possible the data was indexed successfully in Splunk. Kinesis Data Firehose backs up in Amazon S3 data for which the acknowledgement timeout expired."
Splunk.MaxRetriesFailed	"Failed to deliver data to Splunk or to receive acknowledgment. Check your HEC health and try again."
Splunk.ConnectionTimeout	"The connection to Splunk timed out. This might be a transient error and the request will be retried. Kinesis Data Firehose backs up the data to Amazon S3 if all retries fail."
Splunk.InvalidEndpoint	"Could not connect to the HEC endpoint. Make sure that the HEC endpoint URL is valid and reachable from Kinesis Data Firehose."
Splunk.ConnectionClosed	"Unable to send data to Splunk due to a connection failure. This might be a transient error. Increasing the retry duration in your Kinesis Data Firehose configuration might guard against such transient failures."
Splunk.SSLUnverified	"Could not connect to the HEC endpoint. The host does not match the certificate provided by the peer. Make sure that the certificate and the host are valid."
Splunk.SSLHandshake	"Could not connect to the HEC endpoint. Make sure that the certificate and the host are valid."

Amazon Elasticsearch Service Data Delivery Errors

For the Amazon ES destination, Kinesis Firehose sends errors to CloudWatch Logs as they are returned by Elasticsearch.

Lambda Invocation Errors

Kinesis Data Firehose can send the following Lambda invocation errors to CloudWatch Logs.

Error Code	Error Message and Information
Lambda.AssumeRoleAccessDenied	"Access was denied. Ensure that the trust policy for the provided IAM role allows Kinesis Data Firehose to assume the role."
Lambda.InvokeAccessDenied	"Access was denied. Ensure that the access policy allows access to the Lambda function."

Error Code	Error Message and Information
Lambda.JsonProcessingException	"There was an error parsing returned records from the Lambda function. Ensure that the returned records follow the status model required by Kinesis Data Firehose." For more information, see Data Transformation and Status Model.
Lambda.InvokeLimitExceeded	"The Lambda concurrent execution limit is exceeded. Increase the concurrent execution limit." For more information, see AWS Lambda Limits in the *AWS Lambda Developer Guide*.
Lambda.DuplicatedRecordId	"Multiple records were returned with the same record ID. Ensure that the Lambda function returns unique record IDs for each record." For more information, see Data Transformation and Status Model.
Lambda.MissingRecordId	"One or more record IDs were not returned. Ensure that the Lambda function returns all received record IDs." For more information, see Data Transformation and Status Model.
Lambda.ResourceNotFound	"The specified Lambda function does not exist. Use a different function that does exist."
Lambda.InvalidSubnetIDException	"The specified subnet ID in the Lambda function VPC configuration is invalid. Ensure that the subnet ID is valid."
Lambda.InvalidSecurityGroupIDException	"The specified security group ID in the Lambda function VPC configuration is invalid. Ensure that the security group ID is valid."
Lambda.SubnetIPAddressLimitReachedException	"AWS Lambda was not able to set up the VPC access for the Lambda function because one or more configured subnets have no available IP addresses. Increase the IP address limit." For more information, see Amazon VPC Limits - VPC and Subnets in the *Amazon VPC User Guide*.
Lambda.ENILimitReachedException	"AWS Lambda was not able to create an Elastic Network Interface (ENI) in the VPC, specified as part of the Lambda function configuration, because the limit for network interfaces has been reached. Increase the network interface limit." For more information, see Amazon VPC Limits - Network Interfaces in the *Amazon VPC User Guide*.

Accessing CloudWatch Logs for Kinesis Data Firehose

You can view the error logs related to Kinesis Firehose data delivery failure using the Kinesis Firehose console or CloudWatch console. The following procedures show you how to access error logs using these two methods.

To access error logs using the Kinesis Data Firehose console

1. Open the Kinesis Firehose console at https://console.aws.amazon.com/firehose/.

2. On the navigation bar, choose a region.

3. Select a delivery stream name to go to the delivery stream details page.

4. Choose **Error Log** to view a list of error logs related to data delivery failure.

To access error logs using the CloudWatch console

1. Open the CloudWatch console at https://console.aws.amazon.com/cloudwatch/.

2. On the navigation bar, choose a region.

3. In the navigation pane, choose **Logs**.

4. Select a log group and log stream to view a list of error logs related to data delivery failure.

Monitoring Kinesis Agent Health

Kinesis Agent publishes custom CloudWatch metrics with a namespace of **AWSKinesisAgent** to help assess if the agent is healthy, submitting data into Kinesis Data Firehose as specified, and consuming the appropriate amount of CPU and memory resources on the data producer.

Metrics such as number of records and bytes sent are useful to understand the rate at which the agent is submitting data to the Kinesis data delivery stream. When these metrics fall below expected thresholds by some percentage or drop to zero, it could indicate configuration issues, network errors, or agent health issues. Metrics such as on-host CPU and memory consumption and agent error counters indicate data producer resource usage, and provide insights into potential configuration or host errors. Finally, the agent also logs service exceptions to help investigate agent issues.

The agent metrics are reported in the region specified in the agent configuration setting `cloudwatch.endpoint`. For more information, see Agent Configuration Settings.

There is a nominal charge for metrics emitted from Kinesis Agent, which are enabled by default. For more information, see Amazon CloudWatch Pricing.

Monitoring with CloudWatch

Kinesis Agent sends the following metrics to CloudWatch.

Metric	Description
BytesSent	The number of bytes sent to the Kinesis Data Firehose delivery stream over the specified time period. Units: Bytes
RecordSendAttempts	The number of records attempted (either first time, or as a retry) in a call to `PutRecordBatch` over the specified time period. Units: Count
RecordSendErrors	The number of records that returned failure status in a call to `PutRecordBatch`, including retries, over the specified time period. Units: Count
ServiceErrors	The number of calls to `PutRecordBatch` that resulted in a service error (other than a throttling error) over the specified time period. Units: Count

58

Monitoring Amazon Kinesis Data Firehose API Calls with AWS CloudTrail

Amazon Kinesis Data Firehose is integrated with AWS CloudTrail, which captures API calls, delivers the log files to an Amazon S3 bucket that you specify, and maintains API call history. CloudTrail captures API calls made from the Kinesis Data Firehose console or from your code to the Kinesis Data Firehose API. With the information collected by CloudTrail, you can determine the request that was made to Kinesis Data Firehose, the IP address from which the request was made, who made the request, when it was made, and so on.

To learn more about CloudTrail, including how to configure and enable it, see the *AWS CloudTrail User Guide*.

Topics

- Kinesis Data Firehose and CloudTrail History
- Kinesis Data Firehose and CloudTrail Logging
- CloudTrail Log File Entries for Kinesis Data Firehose

Kinesis Data Firehose and CloudTrail History

The CloudTrail API activity history feature lets you look up and filter events captured by CloudTrail. You can look up events related to the creation, modification, or deletion of resources in your AWS account on a per-region basis. Events can be looked up by using the CloudTrail console, or programmatically by using the AWS SDKs or AWS CLI.

The following actions are supported:

- CreateDeliveryStream
- DeleteDeliveryStream
- UpdateDestination

Kinesis Data Firehose and CloudTrail Logging

When CloudTrail logging is enabled in your AWS account, API calls made to specific Kinesis Data Firehose actions are tracked in CloudTrail log files. Kinesis Data Firehose actions are written with other AWS service records. CloudTrail determines when to create and write to a new file based on the specified time period and file size.

The following actions are supported:

- CreateDeliveryStream
- DescribeDeliveryStream
- ListDeliveryStreams
- UpdateDestination
- DeleteDeliveryStream

Every log entry contains information about who generated the request. For example, if a request is made to create a delivery stream (CreateDeliveryStream), the identity of the person or service that made the request is logged. The identity information in the log entry helps you determine the following:

- Whether the request was made with root or IAM user credentials
- Whether the request was made with temporary security credentials for a role or federated user
- Whether the request was made by another AWS service

For more information, see the CloudTrail userIdentity Element.

You can store your log files in your bucket for as long as needed but you can also define Amazon S3 lifecycle rules to archive or delete log files automatically. By default, your log files are encrypted by using Amazon S3 server-side encryption (SSE).

You can have CloudTrail publish SNS notifications when new log files are delivered if you want to take quick action upon log file delivery. For information, see Configuring Amazon SNS Notifications in the *AWS CloudTrail User Guide*.

You can also aggregate Kinesis Data Firehose log files from multiple AWS regions and multiple AWS accounts into a single S3 bucket. For more information, see Receiving CloudTrail Log Files from Multiple Regions and Receiving CloudTrail Log Files from Multiple Accounts in the *AWS CloudTrail User Guide*.

CloudTrail Log File Entries for Kinesis Data Firehose

CloudTrail log files contain one or more log entries. Each entry lists multiple JSON-formatted events. A log entry represents a single request from any source and includes information about the requested action, the date and time of the action, request parameters, and so on. The log entries are not an ordered stack trace of the public API calls, so they do not appear in any specific order.

The following is an example CloudTrail log entry. Note that for security reasons the user name and password for RedshiftDestinationConfiguration will be omitted and returned as an empty string.

```
1  {
2    "Records":[
3        {
4            "eventVersion":"1.02",
5            "userIdentity":{
6                "type":"IAMUser",
7                "principalId":"AKIAIOSFODNN7EXAMPLE",
8                "arn":"arn:aws:iam::111122223333:user/CloudTrail_Test_User",
9                "accountId":"111122223333",
10               "accessKeyId":"AKIAI44QH8DHBEXAMPLE",
11               "userName":"CloudTrail_Test_User"
12           },
13           "eventTime":"2016-02-24T18:08:22Z",
14           "eventSource":"firehose.amazonaws.com",
15           "eventName":"CreateDeliveryStream",
16           "awsRegion":"us-east-1",
17           "sourceIPAddress":"127.0.0.1",
18           "userAgent":"aws-internal/3",
19           "requestParameters":{
20               "deliveryStreamName":"TestRedshiftStream",
21               "redshiftDestinationConfiguration":{
22               "s3Configuration":{
23                   "compressionFormat":"GZIP",
24                   "prefix":"prefix",
25                   "bucketARN":"arn:aws:s3:::firehose-cloudtrail-test-bucket",
26                   "roleARN":"arn:aws:iam::111122223333:role/Firehose",
27                   "bufferingHints":{
28                       "sizeInMBs":3,
29                       "intervalInSeconds":900
30                   },
31                   "encryptionConfiguration":{
32                       "kMSEncryptionConfig":{
33                           "aWSKMSKeyARN":"arn:aws:kms:us-east-1:key"
34                       }
```

60

```
35                    }
36                },
37                "clusterJDBCURL":"jdbc:redshift://example.abc123.us-west-2.redshift.amazonaws.
                      com:5439/dev",
38                "copyCommand":{
39                    "copyOptions":"copyOptions",
40                    "dataTableName":"dataTable"
41                },
42                "password":"",
43                "username":"",
44                "roleARN":"arn:aws:iam::111122223333:role/Firehose"
45            }
46        },
47        "responseElements":{
48            "deliveryStreamARN":"arn:aws:firehose:us-east-1:111122223333:deliverystream/
                  TestRedshiftStream"
49        },
50        "requestID":"958abf6a-db21-11e5-bb88-91ae9617edf5",
51        "eventID":"875d2d68-476c-4ad5-bbc6-d02872cfc884",
52        "eventType":"AwsApiCall",
53        "recipientAccountId":"111122223333"
54    },
55    {
56        "eventVersion":"1.02",
57        "userIdentity":{
58            "type":"IAMUser",
59            "principalId":"AKIAIOSFODNN7EXAMPLE",
60            "arn":"arn:aws:iam::111122223333:user/CloudTrail_Test_User",
61            "accountId":"111122223333",
62            "accessKeyId":"AKIAI44QH8DHBEXAMPLE",
63            "userName":"CloudTrail_Test_User"
64        },
65        "eventTime":"2016-02-24T18:08:54Z",
66        "eventSource":"firehose.amazonaws.com",
67        "eventName":"DescribeDeliveryStream",
68        "awsRegion":"us-east-1",
69        "sourceIPAddress":"127.0.0.1",
70        "userAgent":"aws-internal/3",
71        "requestParameters":{
72            "deliveryStreamName":"TestRedshiftStream"
73        },
74        "responseElements":null,
75        "requestID":"aa6ea5ed-db21-11e5-bb88-91ae9617edf5",
76        "eventID":"d9b285d8-d690-4d5c-b9fe-d1ad5ab03f14",
77        "eventType":"AwsApiCall",
78        "recipientAccountId":"111122223333"
79    },
80    {
81        "eventVersion":"1.02",
82        "userIdentity":{
83            "type":"IAMUser",
84            "principalId":"AKIAIOSFODNN7EXAMPLE",
85            "arn":"arn:aws:iam::111122223333:user/CloudTrail_Test_User",
86            "accountId":"111122223333",
```

```
 87            "accessKeyId":"AKIAI44QH8DHBEXAMPLE",
 88            "userName":"CloudTrail_Test_User"
 89        },
 90        "eventTime":"2016-02-24T18:10:00Z",
 91        "eventSource":"firehose.amazonaws.com",
 92        "eventName":"ListDeliveryStreams",
 93        "awsRegion":"us-east-1",
 94        "sourceIPAddress":"127.0.0.1",
 95        "userAgent":"aws-internal/3",
 96        "requestParameters":{
 97            "limit":10
 98        },
 99        "responseElements":null,
100        "requestID":"d1bf7f86-db21-11e5-bb88-91ae9617edf5",
101        "eventID":"67f63c74-4335-48c0-9004-4ba35ce00128",
102        "eventType":"AwsApiCall",
103        "recipientAccountId":"111122223333"
104    },
105    {
106        "eventVersion":"1.02",
107        "userIdentity":{
108            "type":"IAMUser",
109            "principalId":"AKIAIOSFODNN7EXAMPLE",
110            "arn":"arn:aws:iam::111122223333:user/CloudTrail_Test_User",
111            "accountId":"111122223333",
112            "accessKeyId":"AKIAI44QH8DHBEXAMPLE",
113            "userName":"CloudTrail_Test_User"
114        },
115        "eventTime":"2016-02-24T18:10:09Z",
116        "eventSource":"firehose.amazonaws.com",
117        "eventName":"UpdateDestination",
118        "awsRegion":"us-east-1",
119        "sourceIPAddress":"127.0.0.1",
120        "userAgent":"aws-internal/3",
121        "requestParameters":{
122            "destinationId":"destinationId-000000000001",
123            "deliveryStreamName":"TestRedshiftStream",
124            "currentDeliveryStreamVersionId":"1",
125            "redshiftDestinationUpdate":{
126                "roleARN":"arn:aws:iam::111122223333:role/Firehose",
127                "clusterJDBCURL":"jdbc:redshift://example.abc123.us-west-2.redshift.amazonaws.
                    com:5439/dev",
128                "password":"",
129                "username":"",
130                "copyCommand":{
131                    "copyOptions":"copyOptions",
132                    "dataTableName":"dataTable"
133                },
134                "s3Update":{
135                    "bucketARN":"arn:aws:s3:::firehose-cloudtrail-test-bucket-update",
136                    "roleARN":"arn:aws:iam::111122223333:role/Firehose",
137                    "compressionFormat":"GZIP",
138                    "bufferingHints":{
139                        "sizeInMBs":3,
```

```
140                         "intervalInSeconds":900
141                     },
142                     "encryptionConfiguration":{
143                         "kMSEncryptionConfig":{
144                             "aWSKMSKeyARN":"arn:aws:kms:us-east-1:key"
145                         }
146                     },
147                     "prefix":"arn:aws:s3:::firehose-cloudtrail-test-bucket"
148                 }
149             }
150         },
151         "responseElements":null,
152         "requestID":"d549428d-db21-11e5-bb88-91ae9617edf5",
153         "eventID":"1cb21e0b-416a-415d-bbf9-769b152a6585",
154         "eventType":"AwsApiCall",
155         "recipientAccountId":"111122223333"
156     },
157     {
158         "eventVersion":"1.02",
159         "userIdentity":{
160             "type":"IAMUser",
161             "principalId":"AKIAIOSFODNN7EXAMPLE",
162             "arn":"arn:aws:iam::111122223333:user/CloudTrail_Test_User",
163             "accountId":"111122223333",
164             "accessKeyId":"AKIAI44QH8DHBEXAMPLE",
165             "userName":"CloudTrail_Test_User"
166         },
167         "eventTime":"2016-02-24T18:10:12Z",
168         "eventSource":"firehose.amazonaws.com",
169         "eventName":"DeleteDeliveryStream",
170         "awsRegion":"us-east-1",
171         "sourceIPAddress":"127.0.0.1",
172         "userAgent":"aws-internal/3",
173         "requestParameters":{
174             "deliveryStreamName":"TestRedshiftStream"
175         },
176         "responseElements":null,
177         "requestID":"d85968c1-db21-11e5-bb88-91ae9617edf5",
178         "eventID":"dd46bb98-b4e9-42ff-a6af-32d57e636ad1",
179         "eventType":"AwsApiCall",
180         "recipientAccountId":"111122223333"
181     }
182 ]
183 }
```

Controlling Access with Amazon Kinesis Data Firehose

The following sections cover how to control access to and from your Kinesis Data Firehose resources. The information they cover includes how to grant your application access so it can send data to your Kinesis Data Firehose delivery stream. They also describe how you can grant Kinesis Data Firehose access to your Amazon Simple Storage Service (Amazon S3) bucket, Amazon Redshift cluster, or Amazon Elasticsearch Service cluster, as well as the access permissions you need if you use Splunk as your destination. Finally, you'll find in this topic guidance on how to configure Kinesis Data Firehose so it can deliver data to a destination that belongs to a different AWS account. The technology for managing all these forms of access is AWS Identity and Access Management (IAM). For more information about IAM, see What is IAM?.

Topics

- Grant Your Application Access to Your Kinesis Data Firehose Resources
- Grant Kinesis Data Firehose Access to an Amazon S3 Destination
- Grant Kinesis Data Firehose Access to an Amazon Redshift Destination
- Grant Kinesis Data Firehose Access to an Amazon ES Destination
- Grant Kinesis Data Firehose Access to a Splunk Destination
- VPC Access to Splunk
- Cross-Account Delivery

Grant Your Application Access to Your Kinesis Data Firehose Resources

To give your application access to your Kinesis Data Firehose delivery stream, use a policy similar to this example. You can adjust the individual API operations to which you grant access by modifying the `Action` section, or grant access to all operations with `"firehose:*"`.

```
1  {
2      "Version": "2012-10-17",
3      "Statement": [
4          {
5              "Effect": "Allow",
6              "Action": [
7                  "firehose:DeleteDeliveryStream",
8                  "firehose:PutRecord",
9                  "firehose:PutRecordBatch",
10                 "firehose:UpdateDestination"
11             ],
12             "Resource": [
13                 "arn:aws:firehose:region:account-id:deliverystream/delivery-stream-name"
14             ]
15         }
16     ]
17 }
```

Grant Kinesis Data Firehose Access to an Amazon S3 Destination

When you're using an Amazon S3 destination, Kinesis Data Firehose delivers data to your S3 bucket and can optionally use an AWS KMS key that you own for data encryption. If error logging is enabled, Kinesis Data Firehose also sends data delivery errors to your CloudWatch log group and streams. You are required to have an IAM role when creating a delivery stream. Kinesis Data Firehose assumes that IAM role and gains access to the specified bucket, key, and CloudWatch log group and streams.

Use the following trust policy to enable Kinesis Data Firehose to assume the role. Edit the policy to replace *account-id* with your AWS account ID. This ensures that only you can request Kinesis Data Firehose to assume the IAM role.

```
1  {
2    "Version": "2012-10-17",
3    "Statement": [
4      {
5        "Effect": "Allow",
6        "Principal": {
7          "Service": "firehose.amazonaws.com"
8        },
9        "Action": "sts:AssumeRole",
10       "Condition": {
11         "StringEquals": {
12           "sts:ExternalId":"account-id"
13         }
14       }
15     }
16   ]
17 }
```

Use the following access policy to enable Kinesis Data Firehose to access your S3 bucket and AWS KMS key. If you don't own the S3 bucket, add `s3:PutObjectAcl` to the list of Amazon S3 actions. This grants the bucket owner full access to the objects delivered by Kinesis Data Firehose. This policy also has a statement that allows access to Amazon Kinesis Data Streams. If you don't use Kinesis Data Streams as your data source, you can remove that statement.

```
1  {
2      "Version": "2012-10-17",
3      "Statement":
4      [
5          {
6              "Effect": "Allow",
7              "Action": [
8                  "s3:AbortMultipartUpload",
9                  "s3:GetBucketLocation",
10                 "s3:GetObject",
11                 "s3:ListBucket",
12                 "s3:ListBucketMultipartUploads",
13                 "s3:PutObject"
14             ],
15             "Resource": [
16                 "arn:aws:s3:::bucket-name",
17                 "arn:aws:s3:::bucket-name/*"
18             ]
19         },
20         {
21             "Effect": "Allow",
22             "Action": [
23                 "kinesis:DescribeStream",
24                 "kinesis:GetShardIterator",
25                 "kinesis:GetRecords"
26             ],
27             "Resource": "arn:aws:kinesis:region:account-id:stream/stream-name"
28         },
```

```
29      {
30          "Effect": "Allow",
31          "Action": [
32              "kms:Decrypt",
33              "kms:GenerateDataKey"
34          ],
35          "Resource": [
36              "arn:aws:kms:region:account-id:key/key-id"
37          ],
38          "Condition": {
39              "StringEquals": {
40                  "kms:ViaService": "s3.region.amazonaws.com"
41              },
42              "StringLike": {
43                  "kms:EncryptionContext:aws:s3:arn": "arn:aws:s3:::bucket-name/prefix*"
44              }
45          }
46      },
47      {
48          "Effect": "Allow",
49          "Action": [
50              "logs:PutLogEvents"
51          ],
52          "Resource": [
53              "arn:aws:logs:region:account-id:log-group:log-group-name:log-stream:log-stream-
                    name"
54          ]
55      },
56      {
57          "Effect": "Allow",
58          "Action": [
59              "lambda:InvokeFunction",
60              "lambda:GetFunctionConfiguration"
61          ],
62          "Resource": [
63              "arn:aws:lambda:region:account-id:function:function-name:function-version"
64          ]
65      }
66  ]
67 }
```

For more information about allowing other AWS services to access your AWS resources, see Creating a Role to Delegate Permissions to an AWS Service in the *IAM User Guide*.

Grant Kinesis Data Firehose Access to an Amazon Redshift Destination

Refer to the following when you are granting access to Kinesis Data Firehose when using an Amazon Redshift destination.

Topics

- IAM Role and Access Policy
- VPC Access to an Amazon Redshift Cluster

IAM Role and Access Policy

When you're using an Amazon Redshift destination, Kinesis Data Firehose delivers data to your S3 bucket as an intermediate location. It can optionally use an AWS KMS key you own for data encryption. Kinesis Data Firehose then loads the data from the S3 bucket to your Amazon Redshift cluster. If error logging is enabled, Kinesis Data Firehose also sends data delivery errors to your CloudWatch log group and streams. Kinesis Data Firehose uses the specified Amazon Redshift user name and password to access your cluster, and uses an IAM role to access the specified bucket, key, CloudWatch log group, and streams. You are required to have an IAM role when creating a delivery stream.

Use the following trust policy to enable Kinesis Data Firehose to assume the role. Edit the policy to replace *account-id* with your AWS account ID. This is so that only you can request Kinesis Data Firehose to assume the IAM role.

```
1  {
2    "Version": "2012-10-17",
3    "Statement": [
4      {
5        "Effect": "Allow",
6        "Principal": {
7          "Service": "firehose.amazonaws.com"
8        },
9        "Action": "sts:AssumeRole",
10       "Condition": {
11         "StringEquals": {
12           "sts:ExternalId":"account-id"
13         }
14       }
15     }
16   ]
17 }
```

Use the following access policy to enable Kinesis Data Firehose to access your S3 bucket and AWS KMS key. If you don't own the S3 bucket, add `s3:PutObjectAcl` to the list of Amazon S3 actions, which grants the bucket owner full access to the objects delivered by Kinesis Data Firehose. This policy also has a statement that allows access to Amazon Kinesis Data Streams. If you don't use Kinesis Data Streams as your data source, you can remove that statement.

```
1  {
2  "Version": "2012-10-17",
3      "Statement":
4      [
5          {
6              "Effect": "Allow",
7              "Action": [
8                  "s3:AbortMultipartUpload",
9                  "s3:GetBucketLocation",
10                 "s3:GetObject",
11                 "s3:ListBucket",
12                 "s3:ListBucketMultipartUploads",
13                 "s3:PutObject"
14             ],
15             "Resource": [
16                 "arn:aws:s3:::bucket-name",
17                 "arn:aws:s3:::bucket-name/*"
18             ]
```

```
19          },
20          {
21              "Effect": "Allow",
22              "Action": [
23                  "kms:Decrypt",
24                  "kms:GenerateDataKey"
25              ],
26              "Resource": [
27                  "arn:aws:kms:region:account-id:key/key-id"
28              ],
29              "Condition": {
30                  "StringEquals": {
31                      "kms:ViaService": "s3.region.amazonaws.com"
32                  },
33                  "StringLike": {
34                      "kms:EncryptionContext:aws:s3:arn": "arn:aws:s3:::bucket-name/prefix*"
35                  }
36              }
37          },
38          {
39              "Effect": "Allow",
40              "Action": [
41                  "kinesis:DescribeStream",
42                  "kinesis:GetShardIterator",
43                  "kinesis:GetRecords"
44              ],
45              "Resource": "arn:aws:kinesis:region:account-id:stream/stream-name"
46          },
47          {
48              "Effect": "Allow",
49              "Action": [
50                  "logs:PutLogEvents"
51              ],
52              "Resource": [
53                  "arn:aws:logs:region:account-id:log-group:log-group-name:log-stream:log-stream-
                        name"
54              ]
55          },
56          {
57              "Effect": "Allow",
58              "Action": [
59                  "lambda:InvokeFunction",
60                  "lambda:GetFunctionConfiguration"
61              ],
62              "Resource": [
63                  "arn:aws:lambda:region:account-id:function:function-name:function-version"
64              ]
65          }
66      ]
67 }
```

For more information about allowing other AWS services to access your AWS resources, see Creating a Role to Delegate Permissions to an AWS Service in the *IAM User Guide*.

VPC Access to an Amazon Redshift Cluster

If your Amazon Redshift cluster is in a virtual private cloud (VPC), it must be publicly accessible with a public IP address. Also, grant Kinesis Data Firehose access to your Amazon Redshift cluster by unblocking the Kinesis Data Firehose IP addresses. Kinesis Data Firehose currently uses one CIDR block for each available Region:

- `13.58.135.96/27` for US East (Ohio)
- `52.70.63.192/27` for US East (N. Virginia)
- `13.57.135.192/27` for US West (N. California)
- `52.89.255.224/27` for US West (Oregon)
- `13.228.64.192/27` for Asia Pacific (Singapore)
- `13.210.67.224/27` for Asia Pacific (Sydney)
- `13.113.196.224/27` for Asia Pacific (Tokyo)
- `35.158.127.160/27` for EU (Frankfurt)
- `52.19.239.192/27` for EU (Ireland)

For more information about how to unblock IP addresses, see the step Authorize Access to the Cluster in the *Amazon Redshift Getting Started* guide.

Grant Kinesis Data Firehose Access to an Amazon ES Destination

When you're using an Amazon ES destination, Kinesis Data Firehose delivers data to your Amazon ES cluster, and concurrently backs up failed or all documents to your S3 bucket. If error logging is enabled, Kinesis Data Firehose also sends data delivery errors to your CloudWatch log group and streams. Kinesis Data Firehose uses an IAM role to access the specified Elasticsearch domain, S3 bucket, AWS KMS key, and CloudWatch log group and streams. You are required to have an IAM role when creating a delivery stream.

Use the following trust policy to enable Kinesis Data Firehose to assume the role. Edit the following policy to replace *account-id* with your AWS account ID. This is so that only you can request Kinesis Data Firehose to assume the IAM role.

```
1  {
2    "Version": "2012-10-17",
3    "Statement": [
4      {
5        "Effect": "Allow",
6        "Principal": {
7          "Service": "firehose.amazonaws.com"
8        },
9        "Action": "sts:AssumeRole",
10       "Condition": {
11         "StringEquals": {
12           "sts:ExternalId":"account-id"
13         }
14       }
15     }
16   ]
17 }
```

Use the following access policy to enable Kinesis Data Firehose to access your S3 bucket, Amazon ES domain, and AWS KMS key. If you do not own the S3 bucket, add `s3:PutObjectAcl` to the list of Amazon S3 actions, which grants the bucket owner full access to the objects delivered by Kinesis Data Firehose. This policy also has a statement that allows access to Amazon Kinesis Data Streams. If you don't use Kinesis Data Streams as your data source, you can remove that statement.

```
1  {
```

```
2      "Version": "2012-10-17",
3      "Statement": [
4          {
5              "Effect": "Allow",
6              "Action": [
7                  "s3:AbortMultipartUpload",
8                  "s3:GetBucketLocation",
9                  "s3:GetObject",
10                 "s3:ListBucket",
11                 "s3:ListBucketMultipartUploads",
12                 "s3:PutObject"
13             ],
14             "Resource": [
15                 "arn:aws:s3:::bucket-name",
16                 "arn:aws:s3:::bucket-name/*"
17             ]
18         },
19         {
20             "Effect": "Allow",
21             "Action": [
22                 "kms:Decrypt",
23                 "kms:GenerateDataKey"
24             ],
25             "Resource": [
26                 "arn:aws:kms:region:account-id:key/key-id"
27             ],
28             "Condition": {
29                 "StringEquals": {
30                     "kms:ViaService": "s3.region.amazonaws.com"
31                 },
32                 "StringLike": {
33                     "kms:EncryptionContext:aws:s3:arn": "arn:aws:s3:::bucket-name/prefix*"
34                 }
35             }
36         },
37         {
38             "Effect": "Allow",
39             "Action": [
40                 "es:DescribeElasticsearchDomain",
41                 "es:DescribeElasticsearchDomains",
42                 "es:DescribeElasticsearchDomainConfig",
43                 "es:ESHttpPost",
44                 "es:ESHttpPut"
45             ],
46             "Resource": [
47                 "arn:aws:es:region:account-id:domain/domain-name",
48                 "arn:aws:es:region:account-id:domain/domain-name/*"
49             ]
50         },
51         {
52             "Effect": "Allow",
53             "Action": [
54                 "es:ESHttpGet"
55             ],
```

```
56        "Resource": [
57            "arn:aws:es:region:account-id:domain/domain-name/_all/_settings",
58            "arn:aws:es:region:account-id:domain/domain-name/_cluster/stats",
59            "arn:aws:es:region:account-id:domain/domain-name/index-name*/_mapping/type-name",
60            "arn:aws:es:region:account-id:domain/domain-name/_nodes",
61            "arn:aws:es:region:account-id:domain/domain-name/_nodes/stats",
62            "arn:aws:es:region:account-id:domain/domain-name/_nodes/*/stats",
63            "arn:aws:es:region:account-id:domain/domain-name/_stats",
64            "arn:aws:es:region:account-id:domain/domain-name/index-name*/_stats"
65        ]
66    },
67    {
68        "Effect": "Allow",
69        "Action": [
70            "kinesis:DescribeStream",
71            "kinesis:GetShardIterator",
72            "kinesis:GetRecords"
73        ],
74        "Resource": "arn:aws:kinesis:region:account-id:stream/stream-name"
75    },
76    {
77        "Effect": "Allow",
78        "Action": [
79            "logs:PutLogEvents"
80        ],
81        "Resource": [
82            "arn:aws:logs:region:account-id:log-group:log-group-name:log-stream:log-stream-
                  name"
83        ]
84    },
85    {
86        "Effect": "Allow",
87        "Action": [
88            "lambda:InvokeFunction",
89            "lambda:GetFunctionConfiguration"
90        ],
91        "Resource": [
92            "arn:aws:lambda:region:account-id:function:function-name:function-version"
93        ]
94    }
95    ]
96 }
```

For more information about allowing other AWS services to access your AWS resources, see Creating a Role to Delegate Permissions to an AWS Service in the *IAM User Guide*.

Grant Kinesis Data Firehose Access to a Splunk Destination

When you're using a Splunk destination, Kinesis Data Firehose delivers data to your Splunk HTTP Event Collector (HEC) endpoint. It also backs up that data to the Amazon S3 bucket that you specify, and you can optionally use an AWS KMS key that you own for Amazon S3 server-side encryption. If error logging is enabled, Kinesis Data Firehose sends data delivery errors to your CloudWatch log streams. You can also use AWS Lambda for data transformation.

You are required to have an IAM role when creating a delivery stream. Kinesis Data Firehose assumes that IAM role and gains access to the specified bucket, key, and CloudWatch log group and streams.

Use the following trust policy to enable Kinesis Data Firehose to assume the role. Edit the policy to replace *account-id* with your AWS account ID. This ensures that only you can request Kinesis Data Firehose to assume the IAM role.

```
 1 {
 2   "Version": "2012-10-17",
 3   "Statement": [
 4     {
 5       "Effect": "Allow",
 6       "Principal": {
 7         "Service": "firehose.amazonaws.com"
 8       },
 9       "Action": "sts:AssumeRole",
10       "Condition": {
11         "StringEquals": {
12           "sts:ExternalId":"account-id"
13         }
14       }
15     }
16   ]
17 }
```

Use the following access policy to enable Kinesis Data Firehose to access your S3 bucket. If you don't own the S3 bucket, add `s3:PutObjectAcl` to the list of Amazon S3 actions, which grants the bucket owner full access to the objects delivered by Kinesis Data Firehose. This policy also grants Kinesis Data Firehose access to CloudWatch for error logging and to AWS Lambda for data transformation. The policy also has a statement that allows access to Amazon Kinesis Data Streams. If you don't use Kinesis Data Streams as your data source, you can remove that statement. Kinesis Firehose doesn't use IAM to access Splunk. For accessing Splunk, it uses your HEC token.

```
 1 {
 2     "Version": "2012-10-17",
 3     "Statement":
 4     [
 5         {
 6             "Effect": "Allow",
 7             "Action": [
 8                 "s3:AbortMultipartUpload",
 9                 "s3:GetBucketLocation",
10                 "s3:GetObject",
11                 "s3:ListBucket",
12                 "s3:ListBucketMultipartUploads",
13                 "s3:PutObject"
14             ],
15             "Resource": [
16                 "arn:aws:s3:::bucket-name",
17                 "arn:aws:s3:::bucket-name/*"
18             ]
19         },
20         {
21             "Effect": "Allow",
22             "Action": [
23                 "kms:Decrypt",
```

```
24              "kms:GenerateDataKey"
25          ],
26          "Resource": [
27              "arn:aws:kms:region:account-id:key/key-id"
28          ],
29          "Condition": {
30              "StringEquals": {
31                  "kms:ViaService": "s3.region.amazonaws.com"
32              },
33              "StringLike": {
34                  "kms:EncryptionContext:aws:s3:arn": "arn:aws:s3:::bucket-name/prefix*"
35              }
36          }
37      },
38      {
39          "Effect": "Allow",
40          "Action": [
41              "kinesis:DescribeStream",
42              "kinesis:GetShardIterator",
43              "kinesis:GetRecords"
44          ],
45          "Resource": "arn:aws:kinesis:region:account-id:stream/stream-name"
46      },
47      {
48          "Effect": "Allow",
49          "Action": [
50              "logs:PutLogEvents"
51          ],
52          "Resource": [
53              "arn:aws:logs:region:account-id:log-group:log-group-name:log-stream:*"
54          ]
55      },
56      {
57          "Effect": "Allow",
58          "Action": [
59              "lambda:InvokeFunction",
60              "lambda:GetFunctionConfiguration"
61          ],
62          "Resource": [
63              "arn:aws:lambda:region:account-id:function:function-name:function-version"
64          ]
65      }
66  ]
67 }
```

For more information about allowing other AWS services to access your AWS resources, see Creating a Role to Delegate Permissions to an AWS Service in the *IAM User Guide*.

VPC Access to Splunk

If your Splunk platform is in a VPC, it must be publicly accessible with a public IP address. Also, grant Kinesis Data Firehose access to your Splunk platform by unblocking the Kinesis Data Firehose IP addresses. Kinesis Data Firehose currently uses the following CIDR blocks.

- 18.216.68.160/27, 18.216.170.64/27, 18.216.170.96/27 for US East (Ohio)
- 34.238.188.128/26, 34.238.188.192/26, 34.238.195.0/26 for US East (N. Virginia)
- 13.57.180.0/26 for US West (N. California)
- 34.216.24.32/27, 34.216.24.192/27, 34.216.24.224/27 for US West (Oregon)
- 13.229.187.128/26 for Asia Pacific (Singapore)
- 13.211.12.0/26 for Asia Pacific (Sydney)
- 13.230.21.0/27, 13.230.21.32/27 for Asia Pacific (Tokyo)
- 18.194.95.192/27, 18.194.95.224/27, 18.195.48.0/27 for EU (Frankfurt)
- 34.241.197.32/27, 34.241.197.64/27, 34.241.197.96/27 for EU (Ireland)

Cross-Account Delivery

You can configure your Kinesis Data Firehose delivery stream to deliver data to a destination that belongs to a different AWS account, as long as the destination supports resource-based permissions. For more information about resource-based permissions, see Identity-Based (IAM) Permissions and Resource-Based Permissions. For a list of AWS services that support resource-based permissions, see AWS Services That Work with IAM.

The following procedure shows an example of configuring a Kinesis Data Firehose delivery stream owned by account A to deliver data to an Amazon S3 bucket owned by account B.

1. Create an IAM role under account A using steps described in Grant Kinesis Firehose Access to an Amazon S3 Destination. **Note**
   The Amazon S3 bucket specified in the access policy is owned by account B in this case. Make sure you add s3:PutObjectAcl to the list of Amazon S3 actions in the access policy, which grants account B full access to the objects delivered by Amazon Kinesis Data Firehose.

2. To allow access from the IAM role previously created, create an S3 bucket policy under account B. The following code is an example of the bucket policy. For more information, see Using Bucket Policies and User Policies.

```
1  {
2
3      "Version": "2012-10-17",
4      "Id": "PolicyID",
5      "Statement": [
6          {
7              "Sid": "StmtID",
8              "Effect": "Allow",
9              "Principal": {
10                 "AWS": "arn:aws:iam::accountA-id:role/iam-role-name"
11             },
12             "Action": [
13                 "s3:AbortMultipartUpload",
14                 "s3:GetBucketLocation",
15                 "s3:GetObject",
16                 "s3:ListBucket",
17                 "s3:ListBucketMultipartUploads",
18                 "s3:PutObject",
19                 "s3:PutObjectAcl"
20             ],
21             "Resource": [
22                 "arn:aws:s3:::bucket-name",
23                 "arn:aws:s3:::bucket-name/*"
24             ]
25         }
26     ]
```

74

```
27 }
```

3. Create a Kinesis Data Firehose delivery stream under account A using the IAM role that you created in step 1.

Troubleshooting Amazon Kinesis Data Firehose

You may not see data delivered to your specified destinations. Use the troubleshooting steps in this topic to solve common issues you might encounter while using Kinesis Data Firehose. For further troubleshooting, see Monitoring with CloudWatch Logs.

Topics

- Data Not Delivered to Amazon S3
- Data Not Delivered to Amazon Redshift
- Data Not Delivered to Amazon Elasticsearch Service
- Data Not Delivered to Splunk
- Delivery Stream Not Available as a Target for CloudWatch Logs, CloudWatch Events, or AWS IoT Action

Data Not Delivered to Amazon S3

Check the following if data is not delivered to your S3 bucket.

- Check the Kinesis Data Firehose **IncomingBytes** and **IncomingRecords** metrics to make sure that data is sent to your Kinesis data delivery stream successfully. For more information, see Monitoring with Amazon CloudWatch Metrics.
- If data transformation with Lambda is enabled, check the Kinesis Data Firehose **ExecuteProcessingSuccess** metric to make sure that Kinesis Data Firehose has attempted to invoke your Lambda function. For more information, see Monitoring with Amazon CloudWatch Metrics.
- Check the Kinesis Data Firehose **DeliveryToS3.Success** metric to make sure that Kinesis Data Firehose has attempted putting data to your S3 bucket. For more information, see Monitoring with Amazon CloudWatch Metrics.
- Enable error logging if it is not already enabled, and check error logs for delivery failure. For more information, see Monitoring with Amazon CloudWatch Logs.
- Make sure that the S3 bucket specified in your Kinesis data delivery stream still exists.
- If data transformation with Lambda is enabled, make sure that the Lambda function specified in your delivery stream still exists.
- Make sure that the IAM role specified in your Kinesis data delivery stream has access to your S3 bucket and your Lambda function (if data transformation is enabled). For more information, see Grant Kinesis Data Firehose Access to an Amazon S3 Destination.
- If you're using data transformation, make sure that your Lambda function never returns responses whose payload size exceeds 6 MB. For more information, see Amazon Kinesis Data Firehose Data Transformation.

Data Not Delivered to Amazon Redshift

Check the following if data is not delivered to your Amazon Redshift cluster.

Note that data is delivered to your S3 bucket before loading into Amazon Redshift If the data was not delivered to your S3 bucket, see Data Not Delivered to Amazon S3.

- Check the Kinesis Data Firehose **DeliveryToRedshift.Success** metric to make sure that Kinesis Data Firehose has attempted to copy data from your S3 bucket to the Amazon Redshift cluster. For more information, see Monitoring with Amazon CloudWatch Metrics.
- Enable error logging if it is not already enabled, and check error logs for delivery failure. For more information, see Monitoring with Amazon CloudWatch Logs.
- Check the Amazon Redshift STL_CONNECTION_LOG table to see if Kinesis Data Firehose is able to make successful connections. In this table you should be able to see connections and their status based on a user name. For more information, see STL_CONNECTION_LOG in the *Amazon Redshift Database Developer Guide.*

- If the previous check shows that connections are being established, check the Amazon Redshift STL_LOAD_ERRORS table to verify the reason of the COPY failure. For more information, see STL_LOAD_ERRORS in the *Amazon Redshift Database Developer Guide.*
- Make sure that the Amazon Redshift configuration in your Kinesis data delivery stream is accurate and valid.
- Make sure that the IAM role specified in your Kinesis data delivery stream has access to the S3 bucket from which Amazon Redshift copies data and the Lambda function for data transformation (if data transformation is enabled). For more information, see Grant Kinesis Data Firehose Access to an Amazon S3 Destination.
- If your Amazon Redshift cluster is in a VPC, make sure that the cluster allows access from Kinesis Data Firehose IP addresses. For more information, see Grant Kinesis Data Firehose Access to an Amazon Redshift Destination .
- Make sure that the Amazon Redshift cluster is publicly accessible.
- If you're using data transformation, make sure that your Lambda function never returns responses whose payload size exceeds 6 MB. For more information, see Amazon Kinesis Data Firehose Data Transformation.

Data Not Delivered to Amazon Elasticsearch Service

Check the following if data is not delivered to your Elasticsearch domain.

Note that data can be backed up to your S3 bucket concurrently. If data was not delivered to your S3 bucket, see Data Not Delivered to Amazon S3.

- Check the Kinesis Data Firehose **IncomingBytes** and **IncomingRecords** metrics to make sure that data is sent to your Kinesis data delivery stream successfully. For more information, see Monitoring with Amazon CloudWatch Metrics.
- If data transformation with Lambda is enabled, check the Kinesis Data Firehose **ExecuteProcessing-Success** metric to make sure that Kinesis Data Firehose has attempted to invoke your Lambda function. For more information, see Monitoring with Amazon CloudWatch Metrics.
- Check the Kinesis Data Firehose **DeliveryToElasticsearch.Success** metric to make sure that Kinesis Data Firehose has attempted to index data to the Amazon ES cluster. For more information, see Monitoring with Amazon CloudWatch Metrics.
- Enable error logging if it is not already enabled, and check error logs for delivery failure. For more information, see Monitoring with Amazon CloudWatch Logs.
- Make sure that the Amazon ES configuration in your delivery stream is accurate and valid.
- If data transformation with Lambda is enabled, make sure that the Lambda function specified in your delivery stream still exists.
- Make sure that the IAM role specified in your delivery stream has access to your Amazon ES cluster and Lambda function (if data transformation is enabled). For more information, see Grant Kinesis Data Firehose Access to an Amazon ES Destination.
- If you're using data transformation, make sure that your Lambda function never returns responses whose payload size exceeds 6 MB. For more information, see Amazon Kinesis Data Firehose Data Transformation.

Data Not Delivered to Splunk

Check the following if data is not delivered to your Splunk endpoint.

- Review the Splunk platform requirements. The Splunk Add-on for Kinesis Data Firehose requires Splunk platform version 6.6.X or later. For more information, see Splunk Add-on for Amazon Kinesis Firehose.
- If you have a proxy (Elastic Load Balancing or other) between Kinesis Data Firehose and the HTTP Event Collector (HEC) node, be sure to enable sticky sessions in order to support HEC acknowledgements (ACKs).
- Make sure that you are using a valid HEC token.
- Ensure that the HEC token is enabled. See Enable and disable Event Collector tokens.

- Check to see whether the data that you're sending to Splunk is formatted correctly. See Format events for HTTP Event Collector.
- Make sure that the HEC token and input event are configured with a valid index.
- When an upload to Splunk fails due to a server error from the HEC node, the request is automatically retried. If all retries fail, the data gets backed up to Amazon S3. Check to see if your data appears in Amazon S3, which is an indication of such a failure.
- Make sure that you've enabled indexer acknowledgment on your HEC token. See Enable indexer acknowledgement.
- Increase the value of `HECAcknowledgmentTimeoutInSeconds` in the Splunk destination configuration of your Kinesis Data Firehose delivery stream.
- Increase the value of `DurationInSeconds` under `RetryOptions`in the Splunk destination configuration of your Kinesis Data Firehose delivery stream.
- Check your HEC health.
- If you're using data transformation, make sure that your Lambda function never returns responses whose payload size exceeds 6 MB. For more information, see Amazon Kinesis Data Firehose Data Transformation.
- Make sure that the Splunk parameter named `ackIdleCleanup` is set to `true`. It's false by default. To set this parameter to `true`, do the following:
  - For a managed Splunk Cloud deployment, submit a case using the Splunk Support Portal. In the case, ask Splunk Support to enable the HTTP event collector, set `ackIdleCleanup` to `true` in `inputs.conf`, and create or modify an elastic load balancer to use with this add-on.
  - For a distributed Splunk Enterprise deployment, set the `ackIdleCleanup` parameter to true in the `inputs.conf` file, which is located under `$SPLUNK_HOME/etc/apps/splunk_httpinput/local/` for *nix users and under `%SPLUNK_HOME%\etc\apps\splunk_httpinput\local\` for Windows users.
  - For a single-instance Splunk Enterprise deployment, set the `ackIdleCleanup` parameter to `true` in the `inputs.conf` file, which is located under `$SPLUNK_HOME/etc/apps/splunk_httpinput/local/` for *nix users and under `%SPLUNK_HOME%\etc\apps\splunk_httpinput\local\` for Windows users.
- See Troubleshoot the Splunk Add-on for Amazon Kinesis Firehose.

Delivery Stream Not Available as a Target for CloudWatch Logs, CloudWatch Events, or AWS IoT Action

Some AWS services can only send messages and events to a Kinesis Data Firehose delivery stream that is in the same Region. Verify that your Kinesis Data Firehose delivery stream is located in the same Region as your other services.

Amazon Kinesis Data Firehose Limits

Amazon Kinesis Data Firehose has the following limits.

- By default, each account can have up to 50 Kinesis data delivery streams per Region. If you exceed this limit, a call to CreateDeliveryStream results in a `LimitExceededException` exception. This limit can be increased using the Amazon Kinesis Data Firehose Limits form.

- When **Direct PUT** is configured as the data source, each Kinesis data delivery stream is subject to the following limits:

  - For US East (N. Virginia), US West (Oregon), and EU (Ireland): 5,000 records/second, 2,000 transactions/second, and 5 MiB/second.
  - For US East (Ohio), US West (N. California), Asia Pacific (Singapore), Asia Pacific (Sydney), Asia Pacific (Tokyo), and EU (Frankfurt): 1,000 records/second, 1,000 transactions/second, and 1 MiB/second.

  You can submit a limit increase request using the Amazon Kinesis Data Firehose Limits form. The three limits scale proportionally. For example, if you increase the throughput limit in US East (N. Virginia), US West (Oregon), or EU (Ireland) to 10 MiB/second, the other two limits increase to 4,000 transactions/second and 10,000 records/second. **Important**
  If the increased limit is much higher than the running traffic, it causes very small delivery batches to destinations, which is inefficient and can result in higher costs at the destination services. Be sure to increase the limit only to match current running traffic, and increase the limit further if traffic increases.
  Note
  When Kinesis Data Streams is configured as the data source, this limit doesn't apply, and Kinesis Data Firehose scales up and down with no limit.

- Each Kinesis data delivery stream stores data records for up to 24 hours in case the delivery destination is unavailable.

- The maximum size of a record sent to Kinesis Data Firehose, before base64-encoding, is 1,000 KiB.

- The PutRecordBatch operation can take up to 500 records per call or 4 MiB per call, whichever is smaller. This limit cannot be changed.

- The following operations can provide up to five transactions per second: CreateDeliveryStream, DeleteDeliveryStream, DescribeDeliveryStream, ListDeliveryStreams, and UpdateDestination.

- The buffer sizes hints range from 1 MiB to 128 MiB for Amazon S3 delivery and from 1 MiB to 100 MiB for Amazon Elasticsearch Service (Amazon ES) delivery. For AWS Lambda processing, you can set a buffering hint between 1 MiB and 3 MiB using the https://docs.aws.amazon.com/firehose/latest/APIReference/API_ProcessorParameter.html processor parameter. The size threshold is applied to the buffer before compression. These options are treated as hints, and therefore Kinesis Data Firehose might choose to use different values when it is optimal.

- The buffer interval hints range from 60 seconds to 900 seconds.

- For Kinesis Data Firehose to Amazon Redshift delivery, only publicly accessible Amazon Redshift clusters are supported.

- The retry duration range is from 0 seconds to 7,200 seconds for Amazon Redshift and Amazon ES delivery.

- Kinesis Data Firehose supports Elasticsearch versions 1.5, 2.3, 5.1, 5.3, 5.5, 6.0, and 6.2.

Document History

The following table describes the important changes to the Amazon Kinesis Firehose documentation.

Change	Description	Date Changed
New Kinesis Streams as Source feature	Added Kinesis Streams as a potential source for records for a Firehose Delivery Stream. For more information, see Name and source.	August 18, 2017
Update to console documenatation	The delivery stream creation wizard was updated. For more information, see Creating an Amazon Kinesis Data Firehose Delivery Stream.	July 19, 2017
New data transformation	You can configure Kinesis Data Firehose to transform your data before data delivery. For more information, see Amazon Kinesis Data Firehose Data Transformation.	December 19, 2016
New Amazon Redshift COPY retry	You can configure Kinesis Firehose to retry a COPY command to your Amazon Redshift cluster if it fails. For more information, see Creating an Amazon Kinesis Data Firehose Delivery Stream, Amazon Kinesis Data Firehose Data Delivery, and Amazon Kinesis Data Firehose Limits.	May 18, 2016
New Kinesis Firehose destination, Amazon Elasticsearch Service	You can create a delivery stream with Amazon Elasticsearch Service as the destination. For more information, see Creating an Amazon Kinesis Data Firehose Delivery Stream, Amazon Kinesis Data Firehose Data Delivery, and Grant Kinesis Data Firehose Access to an Amazon ES Destination.	April 19, 2016
New enhanced CloudWatch metrics and troubleshooting features	Updated Monitoring Amazon Kinesis Data Firehose and Troubleshooting Amazon Kinesis Data Firehose.	April 19, 2016
New enhanced Kinesis agent	Updated Writing to Amazon Kinesis Data Firehose Using Kinesis Agent.	April 11, 2016
New Kinesis agents	Added Writing to Amazon Kinesis Data Firehose Using Kinesis Agent.	October 2, 2015

Change	Description	Date Changed
Initial release	Initial release of the Amazon Kinesis Firehose Developer Guide.	October 4, 2015

AWS Glossary

For the latest AWS terminology, see the AWS Glossary in the *AWS General Reference*.

www.ingramcontent.com/pod-product-compliance
Lightning Source LLC
LaVergne TN
LVHW082041050326
832904LV00005B/261